Twenty-Four Aspects
of
Mother Kali

Cover Art: The Primordial Kali.

Digital Imaging by
Prem Durga Marisela Bracho
Editorial and production by
Annapurna/Leigh Anne Gurtov
& Lokelani Kindler

The publication of this book was made possible by assistance
from the Adelaide and Alexander Hixon Foundation
and by donations from friends and students
of the independent SRV Associations.

Sarada Ramakrishna Vivekananda
Associations of Oregon, San Francisco,
New England & Hawaii

Dedication

I offer this work at the Lotus Feet of Mother Kali, the Divine Mother of the Universe, the essence of all gods and goddesses, the Atman existing within all individual beings which is nevertheless inseparable, Who appears as the universe of name and form but Who is simultaneously transcendent of it, Who nurtured me as my earthly father and mother, Who taught me well through my spiritual teachers, Who loves me unconditionally through my wife, friends, family, students and disciples, Who is the boundless ocean of wisdom Who embues thought, word and action with meaning and Who enabled me to gather, organize, express and manifest this book which is reverently offered back to Her.

She is my all. Jai Ma!

Contents

Twenty-Four Aspects
of
Mother Kali

Mother Kali, rising from Lord Shiva's heart,
holding aloft the sword of nondual wisdom,
grasping the severed head of ignorance and egotism,
carrying the skull cup of divine essence
and bearing Shiva's trident.

Her Vision!

The best that life can offer has combined with the most awe-inspiring terror that death is capable of and has assumed a form! Listen! She is of the densest black hue, but what I have seen has turned my hair white for all time! Her abundantly free-flowing locks of raven-colored hair are interminable periods of time, and all regions, divine, terrestrial or hellish, and the myriad forms that inhabit them are helplessly tied there forever, unable to get free! Across this infinite stretch of time and permeating it entirely, Her pervasive blackness reigns, infilling everything as space, both gross and subtle. Her fearsome yet enchanting laughter, rolling inexorably forth like peals of thunder, gives animating motion to all things. Her messengers and attendants, both sublime and terrifying, are entering the cosmic process to do Her bidding, operating a set of powerful laws that defy transcendence.

Yet there is a greater wonder than this, more subtle and endearing. Her momentary glance, falling here and there at perfect intervals, illumines and liberates embodied particles of Her consciousness from all bondage within that terrible web! What to speak of Her glance, Her bewitching smile lights up the three worlds and all attending regions with a radiance so beautiful that Truth Itself bows before Her. Millions of suns and stars, like tiny sparks burning in a black firmament, find at last an object worthy of worship and explode into Her darkness!

I can attest, my friend, that She is no ordinary Divinity! Why else should the God of nondual Wisdom have fallen at Her Feet in speechless amazement! See, He swiftly loses normal consciousness, transported by what He has beheld! And what to wonder, for She has taken His very heart as Her personal abode and dwells there in constant bliss, interminably. Rising from that precious realm, like fragrance from a flower, She fashions the perfect machine of creation, and instills it with life with Her own breath. Behold how She weaves into Her cosmic handicraft multiple twin strands of contrasting opposites, all bound together by the triple forces of nature. Her illusion is insurmountable, for She is the original authoress of creativity and destruction, primeval and eternal.

O Lord! J have seen Her sword of formless Truth flash with infallible accuracy, as by Her design the seas of birth and death swell. She purposefully topples the intricate machinery of manifestation that She created and dissolves all structures reminiscent of form! Countless human heads, centers of awareness free of all bodily attachments, are rolling towards Her Feet, smiles transfixing their faces, their disembodied voices chanting Her many victorious Names. Like marbles in a child's game they obey some unseen force! Mountains of them are rising on all sides, and She stands astride, collecting them like grisly prizes. Rivers of blood from the carnage are pouring into Her open mouth as Her two eyes roll and Her protruding tongue dances here and there! All are returning to Her, are becoming absorbed by Her! All the while Her graceful hands are calming fears and granting inconceivable boons!

The eye at the center of Her forehead is wide open, but none can plumb its depths. Its timeless, spaceless recesses exude an invisible nectar that is palpable but unseen. Under its intoxicating influence all beings are experiencing a transcendent Bliss that is indescribable. Excruciating fear and all-attracting Love are both dissolved in that state, which destroys the very idea of division. In the complete oneness of boundless peace, all comes to rest at last in total unity and the primal Goddess returns to Her own abode, the heart of Shiva, as suddenly as She came, without warning! The "revered spiritual father" who describes this awesome spectacle is no more than a child before Her. Gazing through torrents of blissful tears, he manages to articulate only a few syllables, chanting, 'Aum Ma, Aum Ma, Aum Ma,' over and over again.

Introduction

Eternal salutations to Sri Durga, to Sri Kali, the boundless ocean of spiritual Wisdom who is the Divine Mother of the Universe. This ever-present Goddess epitomizes both the bliss of unlimited Awareness and the enthralling play of universal projection. She manifests countless beings abiding in an infinite set of worlds, seen and unseen, gross and subtle, hidden and exposed. Her existence is confirmed by the holy scriptures, for She is perceived intellectually by means of the Six Darshanas, Her perpetually flowing streams of eternal spiritual knowledge. She is approached and contacted by the devotees through intense sadhana, spiritual disciplines prescribed by the guru, and She is accessible through contemplation and meditation. Ultimately, She is realized as the essence of limitless Consciousness, infinite, indivisible, all-pervading and absolute.

The *Devi*, known as Sri Durga or Sri Kali, is acclaimed throughout the three worlds as the *Deva Devi Svarupaya*, the essence of all gods and goddesses — the ancient, primordial Mother of the Universe whose nature is nondual Truth. She is the primeval Goddess of Wisdom, Sarasvati, whose august name is the oldest existing reference to a

Divine Mother figure in the world's history, appearing in the Vedas many thousands of years before the advent of Christ. She also appears in these eternal scriptures as Uma/Parvati (*Himavat*), the dynamic *shakti* power of Shiva, the God of Wisdom. Under such powerful and time-honored names as Ambika, Lalita, Chandi, Lakshmi, Bhagavati, Narayani and hundreds of others, She makes multiple appearances in the ancient *Puranas* and *Tantras*. In short, She emerges periodically throughout the long march of time, teaching humanity the lessons pertinent to the existence of the immortal Soul (*Atman*) abiding within them.

When speaking about or contemplating Divinity, problems often arise in the human mind with regards to aspect and gender. Is God with form or is God formless? Is Reality male or female, God or Goddess? These questions can only be adequately answered after spiritual realization dawns and the mind is vaulted into nondual, transcendent perception. Until then one should take the affirmative position that perceives Absolute Reality capable of assuming all modes and mediums.

Ultimate Reality cannot be limited or forced to conform to one standard only. It is without limits or boundaries. It must be recognized primarily as the one indivisible Consciousness beyond all names and forms and unaffected by the dualities of the universe and the human mind. If this is understood and accepted at the outset of spiritual life, the appearance of this one aggregate Truth, manifesting through many apparent vehicles — all of them emanations of the One — will pose no problems.

It is after such an understanding has dawned upon the mind that the Divine Mother is seen in all Her glory. The abundant wealth of inspiring names and forms She inhabits cannot exhaust Her qualities and attributes. As Pure Consciousness, homogenous and ever-aware, She transcends the empirical process, yet, as living vibration She also enters into the multidimensional layers of physical matter. It is no wonder that the scriptures indicate Her as *the fundamental power without which the gods could not even lift a finger."* In the *Srimad Devi Bhagavatam,* the great sage Vyasa tells King Janamejaya about Her power:

> *O King! The power of Yogamaya is very great; what shall I speak of Her great power? This whole cosmos is always urged into activity by Her and thus goes rolling on and on incessantly. Even the incarnations are under the influence of Her power and perform their various functions continually.*

The emphasis of this book centers around the condensed essence of these many powers of the Universal Mother. In this regard, Mother Kali represents not only the combined powers inherent in the vast universal plan — the twenty-four Cosmic Principles *(tattvas)* of which the creation is formed (the five elements, the five subtle elements, the five organs of action, the five organs of perception and the mind with its four divisions) — but also the everlasting and abiding Supreme Reality which is immutable and self-effulgent by Its very nature. In both these modes and in every respect, She is infinite. The universe, Her external body (*Prakriti*), reflects this boundlessness to the same degree that the Cosmic Mind, Her internal body (*Hiranyagarbha, Brahma,* etc.), reflects perpetual Intelligence. Both of these worlds, the gross and the subtle, the immanent and the transcendent, exist as component parts of the Divine Mother's essential being called Pure Consciousness, superimposed over It like a sparkling sheen across a glassy surface. Innumerable sets of multidimensional worlds composed of matter and energy get reflected on this eternal foundation of living and timeless Awareness, simultaneously and without cessation. No wonder the devotees of the Universal Mother sing: *"Now can you guess how vast She is? But even this is only a hint!"*

In order to introduce humanity to Her and to convey some idea of Her boundless nature, it is necessary to reveal and discuss some of Her limitless attributes and Divine qualities. This process proceeds under the assumption that the Divine Mother of the Universe — the true Mother of all living beings, their eternal Source and the essence of their very existence — has been forgotten, Her ineffable presence somehow overlooked. This oversight, this loss of memory is tragic and the cause of great suffering and misery among the inhabitants of the world. Being the greatest misfortune, it is also an unexplainable phenomenon, for who indeed could be so careless as to forget their own mother, what to speak of the Mother of all souls? Only those beset with chronic spiritual amnesia could be so forlorn as to arrive at such a truly lamentable condition. Ramprasad Sen, the great Bengali poet and devotee of the Divine Mother sings of this inconceivable loss in one of his wisdom songs:

> O human mind,
> throughout your thinking process
> invoke the subtle sound of Kali, Kali, Kali.
> Why not ground your entire being
> in Her Holy Name,
> which dissolves all dangers arising from without
> and from within?
> How can you forget, even for an instant,
> Her supremely precious Name?
> The mind that remembers the Mother
> experiences no fear when facing the terrible
> expanse of universal suffering.
>
> Overcome with fervent love, this poet pleads:
> 'O mind, how can you possibly forget the
> Mother? At the very center of your being
> sing ceaselessly the Name of Kali,
> for your life in the current of time
> is coming to an end.'[1]

The *Twenty-Four Aspects of Mother Kali*, then, represent in book form an attempt to remind humanity of their divine parentage, of their divine nature, of their source of origin. It is hoped that those who are still asleep to this supreme verity called the Divine Mother of the Universe will have their inherent spirituality awakened; that those who have fallen into complacency or despondency will have their commitment to this nondual Truth of existence rekindled; that those who are already abiding in this Truth will further exult in this sublime Essence of pure Being and continue to spread the pure light of Timeless Awareness to all inhabitants sporting consciously or unconsciously in the boundless ocean of the Universal Mother's ineffable Grace.

Babaji Bob Kindler
SRV Associations of the West
Hawaii
July 4th, 1995

The Four Arms of Goddess Kali

Varada Mudra ~ The Gift of Immortal Life
Abhaya Mudra ~ Fear's Greatest Fear
Sword of Wisdom ~ The Separator that Unifies
Severed Head ~ The Demise of Ignorance

A tremendous amount of Mother Kali's abundant life-transforming force is represented by Her four lovely yet powerful arms. Her upper left arm lofts the sword of nondual wisdom, ready to remove the impositions of ignorance. Her lower left arm presents to our view the stunning spectacle of a severed head, dripping with the blood of sacrifice and self-surrender. It symbolizes the destruction of selfish clinging to mundane objects and considerations and the complete offering of the mind and all its hopes, thoughts and aspirations. The upper right arm is raised in a threatening yet protective manner, hand positioned in *Abhaya Mudra,* a mystic gesture indicating the Divine Mother's serious warning to negative forces that may attempt to harm Her precious spiritual children. Her lower right hand is also poised in a mystic gesture, sporting a *Varada Mudra,* signifying the free and gracious offering of all manner of boons and gifts to those who approach Her for refuge. As the sword and the severed head are closely interconnected, their symbology will be dealt with later in this chapter. The two arms with their respective mudras will be explored and discussed first.

Questions inevitably arise with regards to the many-armed deities filling the ranks of the Hindu pantheon of gods and goddesses. Several diverse meanings apply to each and every divine manifestation according to their character or personality. The general and overall significance of the many-armed stereotype, however, reflects the qualities of pervasiveness, penetration and potency. With the example of Mother Kali, the four arms indicate that Her powers are at work throughout the universe, perpetrating every act and deed. All hands do Her bidding, all muscles exert to accomplish Her comprehensive work. Many other appendages function similarly, for millions of legs carry countless bodies, all containing Her subtle awareness, to the farthest reaches of Her creation. In this regard, She is truly the Mother of the Universe, the practical and consummate *Vashishtadvaitan,* first forming and creating the world of name and form out of the materials of nature *(Prakriti)* and then entering into them all as animating Consciousness *(Shakti-chaitanya).* Her four arms, then, are intrinsically connected with the act of self-surrender, for those who meditate upon Her with one-pointed devotion realize Her extreme power and potency and offer themselves wholeheartedly. They know Her will to be supreme. She fills the void with all types of conscious life-forms and creates a universe engaged in divine sport, and this She accomplishes from Her characteristically detached attitude.

For those who recognize Her everywhere, existing in everything, thoughts of personal will and individual existence prove to be phantoms, as illusory as the limited state of mind that enforces them. They are superimpositions over Reality, which is always homogenous and indivisible, perfect and eternal. In the light of this realization, the mind's ideas regarding diversity, including all that troubles the earth and its creatures, become transformed. A sense of integral connection and cohesiveness then pervades all modes of existence. The illumined beings who are cognizant of this truth of unity perceive only one conscious force in the universe and recognize its diverse manifestations as representations of a consummate whole. The ignorant see only a sporadic and unrelated series of coincidences. In one of Swami Vivekananda's masterful poems, this truth is communicated aptly:

> *They know not Truth,*
> *who dream such vacant dreams*
> *as father, mother, children, wife and friend.*
> *The sexless Self, whose father He? Whose child?*
> *Whose friend, whose foe is He who is but One.*
> *The Self is all and all, none else exists.*
> *And thou art That...*[2]

Later in the same poem, he expresses this Truth from an ultimate standpoint:

> *There is but One —*
> *The Free — The Knower — Self!*
> *Without a name, without a form or stain.*
> *In Him is Maya, dreaming all this dream.*

The Witness, He appears as nature, soul.
Know Thou art That...[3]

It is this nondual atmosphere that the Universal Mother's four arms epitomize, but it is not a sterile and lifeless unity of amorphous indistinction and tired conformity. The old and worn out concepts of what true nondual experience consists of are shattered by Her appearance on the contemporary world scene. This has been fully demonstrated by the birth of Her emanations, Sri Ramakrishna Paramahamsa and Sri Sarada Devi, in recent times. Through these two beings, the Eternal Divine Couple, Mother Kali has revealed that *Brahman* and *Shakti* are indivisible and that true nondual experience is ever present and always attainable to the aspiring soul. The four physical arms of Sarada-Ramakrishna represent Mother Kali's spiritual power at work in the universe. The inner accomplishments and transforming presence of the Divine Couple have laid the foundation for the emergence of a unified world based upon spiritual truths. Swami Vivekananda sings of Them in one of his wonderful devotional songs: *"The leader of souls, Sri Ramakrishna, is born again on earth! He who once uttered the eternal message of the Bhagavad Gita on the battlefield of Kurukshetra with a voice like a lion's roar."* After revealing the RadhaKrishna of this age, the famous swami identifies Them as Mother Sita and Sri Rama as well: *"Behold, Sita's beloved has returned again!"*[4]

The union of Shiva and Shakti produces more

intensity than concepts regarding form and form-lessness can possibly express. When Mother Kali's arms of divinely ordained dynamic action and ecstatic creative sport join with Lord Shiva's arms of inner bliss and transcendent perfection, who can conceive of what may transpire! Certainly, when Mother Kali springs from Her eternal abode in Lord Shiva's heart, like perfume wafting from a flower, the perfection inherent in Her cosmic dance is not altered in the least by the appearance of the world of name and form. The demons of negativity, those illusions of deranged and misguided minds, are misconceptions nurtured in beings who lose their divinely gifted insight, bartering it for paltry possessions such as the sense of ownership, the desire for individual existence and enjoyment of the diverse world that spreads out before them. Fragmenting this inseparable kingdom into many parts, they lord and war over minute portions of it, considering the entire creation as their personal domain. In this way does the birth and continuation of delusion perpetuate itself.

Apart from these many privately owned hells, and fully independent of all such limiting and illusory constrictions, lies the eternal land of true peace and lasting happiness. This is a vast and boundless expanse of sublime experience, not limited by the appearance of name and form but not separate from it either. It is not a land stripped of glory and left sterile and devoid of substance, nor does it resemble the descriptions given by nihilistic philosophers who assert that the realm of nondual perception is a vacuum or a void. This is the realm of Pure Consciousness, capable of formulation and distillation but thoroughly fluid and of the very nature of homogeneity. It transcends and defies all attempts to describe or limit It. It is not restricted to association with changing phenomena, yet changelessness is not Its essential nature either. Both fluctuation and immutability are modes which It enters alternately and freely at will. Imagine the bliss of an indivisible Awareness that merges the collective experiences of all beings within It while still maintaining the ability to witness their origin, existence and dissolution. Such an ineffable condition, though it can scarcely be described, is indicated by the Divine Mother's quartet of arms, raised benignly and powerfully to indicate both the existence and the merging of all extremes. To reach a mature understanding of the Mother's consummate condition, it is necessary to take each of Her divine arms as subjects for separate study.

Varada Mudra – The Gift of Immortal Life

The Varada Mudra, the benign position that the Divine Mother is assuming with Her lower right hand, is the ultimate assurance that anyone could ever receive. Generally associated with the conferring of boons, this mudra is actually a transmission of essential well-being, transferring a strong sense of the deepest security and the most profound peace. Such serenity rarely accompanies life, with its difficult extremes and vicissitudes, so it is a great relief to receive such a gift. Those who gain this vision of excellence move through life with grace and ease, supported and protected by the unfailing radiance emanating from the Universal Mother's sweet beneficence.

The Varada Mudra is fully positive and grants whatever the Mother deems most suitable for the devotee at any given point in worldly and spiritual evolution. The offering of boons is a function of Her generous nature coupled with comprehensive wisdom, for She always knows what is best for Her precious children. When the Mother shows Her child the efficacious Varada Mudra, its effects extend through all realms of being — physical, vital, mental and spiritual. The mudra also grants the attainment of diverse gifts, from small needs to important acquisitions. The pertinent needs of every temperament are then met with and satisfied in proper fashion, for She is the fulfiller of all desires for Her devotees.

In this way has Mother Kali become known as the *Kalpataru* (wish-fulfilling tree), for She is the bestower of the famous *Purusharthas,* or Four Fruits of Life. *Dharma* (righteous living), *Artha* (right livelihood) and *Kama* (satisfaction of desires), all become accessible to living beings according to their inherent karmas coupled with Her mindful scrutiny and Grace. The fourth fruit, *Moksha* (spiritual emancipation), is reserved for those who have learned the lessons of earthly life, especially those pertaining to the transitory nature of limited existence and the need to transcend relativity.

For those who are extremely devoted and seek Truth without compromise, She bestows upon them the most precious treasures of liberation and pure Love for God. These are the rarest achievements, only partially attainable by personal self-effort. Both of them, spiritual emancipation and selfless love of God, are transmitted via the Universal Mother's Varada Mudra, Her own Grace manifested for deserving beings. It is said that the Lord grants all measure of good upon living beings if they but turn to Him, but He is loath to grant pure Love so easily. This is because few love for Love's sake alone. Most all beings love for various self-motivated reasons. The sacrifice of all personal considerations with regard to body and mind is a rare thing, seen only occasionally among the most dedicated of beings. Genius is attended by this kind of dedication, but it is usually associated only with the intellectual attainments of the world. One-pointed absorption into matters of a spiritual nature is accessible only to those whom the Mother graces with mature detachment and complete fulfillment. For such as these, the Varada Mudra holds the supreme blessing.

Abhaya Mudra — Fear's Greatest Fear

The *Abhaya Mudra* is a sign by which Mother Kali confers complete fearlessness upon Her votaries. Its twofold significance conveys the Mother's wish that all beings become courageous through their own efforts and realize Her assurance that there is no ultimate fear possible in Her presence. The message of fearlessness is one of the single most important issues with regards to the spiritual life of aspiring beings and has considerable significance within the context of life in the world as well. In this ocean of potential human misery, the Mother's presence steers the craft of the body/mind mechanism across the sea of worries and dangers, guiding it deftly through the gigantic waves of birth and death. In this way, She is the polestar of our life by which we are able to navigate the stormy tracts of universal suffering involving karmic propensities and precarious human relations. Refuge in Her acts as both an ultimate remedy for all internal ailments and an impenetrable shield against exterior dangers.

The dangers which come upon living beings from the outside are forces of a negative influence. Mother Kali is supremely suited to deal with these types of forces and is unrelenting in Her pursuit and destruction of them. Naive beings whose faith in spiritual matters is still growing, pose prime targets for these antagonistic powers. As long as human beings proceed to focus their physical, vital and mental energies upon mundane matters and superficial preoccupations, so long do the negative forces allow them to function, for their attentions are primarily concerned with the material world and its fundamental considerations. As soon as higher aspirations make their appearance in the human heart, however, obstacles and difficulties spring up as if from nowhere. These are puzzling and perplexing in nature and are often virtually untraceable to any set source or cause. Taking refuge in the Mother's Abhaya Mudra facilitates release from these persistent problems and reveals that a courageous stance is necessary for spiritual growth. The mudra of protection also applies to the realm of personal dilemmas. Often, subtle and unseen problems prove the most difficult to remove, since locating and identifying them seems impossible. Repercussions from long forgotten past actions, stagnation due to trepidation and lack of confidence, knots in the mental and emotional parts of the being due to inherent negative impressions — these and other barriers inhibiting the advance of progress are struck down swiftly and completely by taking sincere refuge in Mother Kali.

She is incomparable in Her representation of perfection and inexorable in Her drive to make it accessible to Her dedicated children. Her path is void of compromise and all imperfections must be vanquished from human consciousness. This is why beings of weak character and mediocre substance vacillate to a more congenial and acquiescent ideal, unable to bear the force of transformation or unwilling to submit to the precise method which Goddess Kali reveals and advises. Only those wholly dedicated to Truth and serious about removing all impediments in the way of attaining It will subject their minds to the fire of purification inherent in the path of the Divine Mother. Absolute perfection and immersion into Divine Reality represents the only goal worth having to such as these. Therefore, it is their recourse to the Four Arms of Goddess Kali that makes absorption possible.

The Four Arms of Goddess Kali are actually one in essence. By restricting all negativity with the power of Her Abhaya Mudra while inviting all courageous aspirants to come forth to receive the precious boons of peace, happiness and freedom inherent in Her Varada Mudra, the Divine Mother simultaneously neutralizes all difficulties and harmonizes all extremes. It is the perfect combination — peace through fearlessness, happiness through refuge, fulfillment through self-surrender. What then of the shining sword and the severed head resting in Her remaining two hands?

The Sword of Wisdom — *The Separator that Unifies*

The sword of nondual wisdom and the severed head of ignorance represent spiritual growth and its accomplishment. Purification of human nature is necessary before the boons of fearlessness and success can be attained. Therefore, Mother Kali captivates our attention with this dynamic spectacle. A swift end to suffering and imposition is the way of Goddess Kali. There is no compromise or complacency allowed for Her devotees. Inside of one lifetime, all impediments to the mind's illumination will be destroyed and the realization of the Self in all (*Atman*) will be actualized.

The sword of wisdom brings this actualization to bear swiftly and in a fashion characteristic of the way of the Universal Mother. This powerful tool is called "the separator that unifies," and not without good reason, for the downward arc of the Divine Mother's sword of wisdom causes a permanent separation of what is illusory from that which is true and substantial. The various delusions and half-truths inhabiting the mind accustomed to certain archaic beliefs and misconceptions simply cannot survive the sword's keen cutting edge. After they are isolated from what is permanent and abiding, they lose their foundation and get systematically dissolved. This carving away of complex mental knots and perplexing appearances and the resultant revelation of Truth is the purpose for the sword's existence and its primary function. Thus does the famous and ancient Vedantic adage, *"Brahman is the only Reality,"* get fulfilled time and time again as the sword of nondual wisdom destroys what is unreal and exposes what is real.

The Divine Mother loves to sport in the diverse world of polar opposites and it is Her desire that all beings play there for a time as well. In the event that attachment to the limited enjoyment of the body/mind condition becomes overwhelming and the *jiva* (embodied soul) finds itself trapped in relativity, the sword of wisdom then severs the root of obsessive human nature, destroying all tendencies to cling to mundane existence. The loss of what one is habituated to leaves a void which needs filling. To compensate, the Divine Mother graciously replaces this emptiness with a return to the original condition of inherent knowing. This softens the abrupt shock of nondual realization and rekindles the remembrance of the jiva's pristine nature — a verity which is deathless and timeless. Mundane attachment then swiftly becomes a vague dream of the past, easily forgotten in the blissful equipoise of residing in the *Atman*, the eternal Self of all beings.

It is not merely inadvertent attachment to things mundane that poses a serious danger to spiritual life. Besides the superficial attractions and aversions of physical existence and the desires and obsessions of the dual mind, there is also the presence of negativities. According to ancient wisdom, these are of three kinds: external, having to do with dangers present in everyday life in the world; internal, concerning the emergence of many detrimental impressions arising from the subconscious mind; and distorting influences from higher powers that strive to utilize living beings for their own ends. Here too, the Divine Mother's wisdom sword saves and liberates, acting to protect precious life forms from untimely disasters. The same shining weapon which enlivens mundane existence, destroys superficiality and puts an end to complacency, also shields living beings from all types of dangers.

Finally, a myriad of profound and meaningful experiences awaits the aspiring soul that ponders the boundless nature of indivisible Consciousness. The sharp edge of the wisdom sword does not cease to function at this lofty level either, but continues to cut away any subtle coverings that would obscure the blazing light of Truth. For the enlightened being, then, the sword of wisdom is not merely an instrument for getting rid of ignorance — an illusion no longer applicable to them — but is also a self-effulgent principle which lights the corridors leading to the highest nondual experience and reveals the radiant expanse of Absolute Reality. It is no wonder that the Wisdom Mother holds it high above, in the atmosphere of transcendence, and keeps it ready to strike at the very heart of selfish clinging, mundane convention and cosmic superimposition.

The Severed Head – The Demise of Ignorance

The severed head of ignorance is the result of the Mother's unerring skill and expertise at rooting out what is weak, shallow and unworthy in Her devotees. However, She does not claim this grisly prize by imposing Her will upon human beings. Our ignorance must be recognized and offered before She will apply Her precise skill of subtle surgery. If this is accomplished, She will willingly and mercilessly relieve us of imperfections arising from ignorance which springs from the lack of knowledge of our true nature.

For those who can bear the fire of purification and who sincerely desire to be free from limitation, Mother Kali demonstrates the skill of an adept surgeon by cutting out exactly what is problematic in our nature, leaving all other areas untouched and free to grow and expand. The smile and distant gaze imprinted upon the face of the severed head in Her hand reveals that all suffering and misery have been eradicated from the physical, vital, mental and spiritual parts of human nature — that the death of the rascal ego has been accomplished. The crimson blood that flows from the now peaceful appendage symbolizes the destruction of attachment to body-consciousness, the demise of the ego and the leaking away of its power over the human mind. The severed head itself indicates that ignorance is of the mind alone, and that true happiness is achieved forever when self-surrender to God is affected.

The Fours Arms of the Goddess present a consummate picture. The Divine Mother is saying:

> *Come to me (Varada Mudra) and offer yourself to Me (Severed Head) and I will protect you from all dangers (Abhaya Mudra) by granting you refuge at My Feet (Varada Mudra). Give yourself completely (Severed Head) to My path of perfection by practicing disciplines (Abhaya Mudra) for purification (Sword of Wisdom) and I will remove all dangers (Abhaya Mudra) and grant liberation (Varada Mudra) by destroying ignorance (Sword of Wisdom) in your mind (Severed Head).*

5

Her Wisdom Eye

The Inscrutable Gaze of Infinity

Adding immense character to the already striking visage of Mother Kali, the wisdom eye, or third eye as it is known, appears above Her dark eyebrows at the center of Her lovely forehead. Like a single radiant star cast upon a dense, black firmament, this strange phenomenon holds powerful significance. Its stunning presence on the Universal Mother's beautiful face not only captivates the attention, but hints at mystical secrets totally unknown to the aspiring minds of humanity.

Perhaps no other quality speaks so clearly and endearingly about the presence of Truth than the Mother's wisdom eye. The revered and blessed Jesus Christ of Nazareth spoke of such a phenomenon when He stated that to see the Father, *"thine eye must be single."* Such inferences point positively to the indivisible nature of Reality and lead us towards perception of the unification of all existence.

The human organism sports two of everything — arms, hands, legs, feet, eyes, ears, nostrils, etc. Duality is imprinted upon our very appearance. Even our minds are dual, seldom striving and always failing to reach the focused and balanced plateau of peaceful existence. It is a wondrous thing, then, that the Mother of our souls possesses this key to unity that unlocks the doorway of perfect Freedom. Truth, unity and freedom — these are the eternal qualities symbolized by Mother Kali's eye of wisdom.

These three immutable attributes all indicate Omniscience. The function of an eye is to see, and in the case of Goddess Kali, Her boundless gaze extends far into infinity. She knows past, present and future, for they are all wrapped up nicely in Her tight universal package called space, time and causation (*desha, kala, nimitta*). She is free — free to close Her single eye in supernal sleep that at once places the entire universe in a state of dissolution, or close It in a profound meditation so deep and insightful as to make the combined realizations of the gods and goddesses seem insignificant. Or She can open Her third eye and project an entire universe in an instant, for Her awakening animates consciousness and brings it to bear in all beings abiding throughout all spheres of existence.

Her wisdom eye perceives intimately all things in the universe and penetrates beyond into the formless region as well. If fully illumined beings, while plunged in sacred vision, behold Her eye of Truth in an open position, this indicates that Her wisdom teachings are accessible to all who are sincere and that the path to the realization of the Atman lies open. If they perceive that Her eye is half-closed, a sleep of ignorance is cast over the minds of creatures and the path of spiritual ascent is steep and filled with obstacles. Finally, if the wisdom eye is seen to be completely closed, *Pralaya*, the dissolution of the universe, is at hand, which puts an end to the manifestation of the worlds of name and form and all their expressions. At this time, the universe remains in seed form, existing subtly in the vast and pure mind of Mother Kali as dormant ideas and concepts.

Expressed in another way, an open eye indicates the opportunity for growth in an atmosphere conducive to spiritual awakening. A half-closed eye indicates an age containing a mixture of knowledge and ignorance — a time when beings must struggle hard to overcome the effects of ignorance and the bondage that results from it. A closed eye puts an end to all ideas of growth or progress. At this time, the illumined are merged in Her while the unillumined await the manifestation of the next cosmic cycle, their energies lying latent, contained and involved within the potential ideas and creative concepts occupying Her fertile mind.

The cosmic mind of Mother Kali contains the Fourteen Spheres of Existence and is the terrain upon which all of them — seven upper and seven lower — have their foundation. Each "sphere" is actually a gradated realm of existence containing thousands of worlds, where life-forms live their lives according to their inherent destinies. Through them all, the wisdom eye penetrates, manifesting as the very principle of light. Light enables the eye to see and therefore is its inherent property. In the physical worlds, Her eye is represented by the sun in the sky, casting radiance upon all who abide there. None could live or see without Her warmth and brilliance. In a realm consisting of subtler materials, where the senses and the physical objects they perceive are not needed, Her eye is the light of pure intelligence that reveals and supports the higher truths existing there.

Her omniscience, then, reveals all that needs to be seen or known. It casts a light upon physical worlds and illumines matters of the mind as well. That Her eye is positioned in the middle of the forehead reveals the mind and its powers to be of great importance. An opening of the third eye, called the *Ajna chakra* in the science of *Kundalini Yoga,* is the boon bestowed upon one whom the Divine Mother wishes to awaken to inner mystical experiences. It indicates that the contents of the mind are becoming refined and purified, that obstacles to subtle insight are being removed and that enlightenment of the entire being is approaching.

When the Divine Mother awakens the third eye of wisdom in Her devotee, entire realms of mystic experience are opened up. Visions of celestial regions and the presiding deities that inhabit them are not uncommon. With the mind taken up in periods of blissful absorption, interest in mundane matters having to do with the ordinary world, decreases. The mind then realizes that time and space are relative concepts, having sway only over those minds which choose to relegate their consciousness to narrow constrictions. Letting go of old notions pertaining to time and locale, and diverting the mind's attention from the interminable rounds of mundane ritual which constitutes the daily activities of the worldly-minded who are obsessed with sensuality and materiality, the fortunate awakened soul plunges into experiences of unalloyed bliss. Hours, days and months of supernal contemplation pass by and flow onward, finally culminating in total immersion with the source of existence.

The characteristics of beings who experience these mystical states reflect both power and depth of knowledge. Prolonged and continual access to this sixth center of consciousness brings profound illumination to the entire being, resulting finally in the experience of *Nirvikalpa Samadhi* — a nondual state of complete absorption into Absolute Reality. It is at this juncture of human evolution that the eye truly becomes single and the origin and true nature of Consciousness becomes revealed. This is the ultimate function and significance of the Universal Mother's wisdom eye. Though it represents physical light to those living in relativity, clarifies the understanding of those seeking intellectual knowledge, brings deeper insight to all who dwell in astral and causal realms, and acts as a tool for spiritual awakening among the seekers of higher Truth, its main purpose is consummated at the nondual level where the individual soul merges with the Supreme Soul. In this way does it function as a doorway into the seventh center of highest Consciousness called the *Sahashrara,* where all distinctions vanish and limitations no longer apply.

The wisdom eye sees all and is aware of every occurrence and manifestation, yet remains ever focused on nondual Truth. In this way it draws all diversity towards the ultimate and predestined goal of complete unification. If its subtle presence were unknown, the realms of higher learning pertaining to spiritual sciences would be inaccessible to human beings. Indeed, this condition is now prevalent on earth in this age, as few even believe in Supreme Truth or Divine Reality. Many of those who profess to be aware of higher consciousness are either participating in stylish fads or creating businesses to profit from the gullibility of human nature. Truth has nothing to do with trends which come and go such as magic and occult practices, nor does it get revealed through various money-making schemes. Only those rare and intrepid spiritual wayfarers who would shatter the illusion of time, space and causation and behold Reality face to face can understand and experience pure Consciousness. Only they are aware of the intense commitment necessary to realize God and know that Reality is beyond the mere posturings of believing or nonbelieving.

The wisdom eye is not just a symbol or a far-fetched theory. It is a subtle pathway for refined consciousness to rise beyond the sense-bound mind. Nor is the Divine Mother Kali just a fantastic image of the imagination or even a comprehensive symbol for Reality. She is the formless Reality without a second, as well as the living, breathing energy of consciousness that appears as the animating force inhabiting all names and forms. Thought and matter are both Her creations, yet She can transcend them at will. Her own eye of wisdom is the archetype, the authentic original, the Light of lights by which others perceive. The prayer of all enlightened beings is that She may open Her wisdom eye and cast Its Truth-glance upon all beings so that freedom and unity may become the fundamental standards of life once again!

6

Mother Kali's Lotus Feet

Twin Saviors that Liberate

Like effulgent purple lotuses of royal hue, the Universal Mother's feet of refuge pervade the realm of life and death, floating like sturdy lifeboats on the stormy sea of relative existence. The soles of Her feet of redeeming grace are tinged with brilliant red to attract and save struggling beings given to intense activity and bound by its effects. The lotus feet represent the very foundation of Divine Mother Reality, and extend upwards through the terrestrial worlds into heights of spiritual splendor far beyond physical limitations, finally merging with the vast, boundless expanse of pure Consciousness.

The consummate meditator reaches perfection using strict discrimination followed by mature renunciation resulting in complete affirmation. What is more, this total and committed discipline must proceed by an act of personal will that is guided, focused and adjusted by an illumined preceptor. This spiritual influence in human form will often give instructions pertinent to time, place and temperament, starting the aspirant on the gradual ascent towards realization by helping establish a firm foundation. No foundation is stronger than refuge in the Universal Mother, who is the dynamic power of the Absolute, identical with It. Thus it is said that the lotus feet of the Mother are indispensable to those who undertake the precarious practices necessary for progress in sadhana and spiritual life.

The one known as the Divine Mother is intrinsically real and concerned for all beings. A contemporary emanation of Divine Mother power in this present day and age is found in Sri Sarada Devi, known as the Holy Mother. She has introduced many powerful teachings for those proceeding along the pathway towards perfection. With regards to refuge in God, the basis and prerequisite of all spiritual practice, Her advice is clear:

> *One must practice disciplines at least in the morning and the evening. Such practice acts like the rudder of a boat. When a person sits in the evening for prayer, he can reflect on the good and bad things he did in the course of the day. Next, while performing Japa, he should meditate on his Chosen Ideal. In meditation he should first think of the face of his Chosen Deity, but then should meditate on the entire body from the feet upward.*[5]

Thus, for those who select the Divine Mother as their chosen ideal, Her lotus feet will occupy a position of great importance, especially at the outset of spiritual life. Taking sincere refuge in the primordial Mother of the Universe is the wisest decision, for Her guidance is infallible. Why should one take the feet of the Mother before setting sail upon the vast sea of inner awareness? The Holy Mother, Sri Sarada Devi, again provides the answer:

*Nothing whatsoever is ever achieved unless
Mahamaya clears the path. A person's brain
becomes deranged if they force themselves into
excessive prayer and meditation. The intelligence of a man is very precarious. It is like the
head of a screw. If one thread is loosened then he
goes crazy. Or he becomes entangled in the trap
of Mahamaya and thinks himself to be quite all
right. But if the screw is tightened in a different
direction, one follows the right path and enjoys
peace and happiness.*

Complete and absolute surrender under the protection of the Supreme Being is the inner significance of Mother Kali's dark blue lotus feet. Refuge
and protection, guidance and sustenance, peace and
happiness are all attained by this powerful act of
giving. Like the severed head in the Mother's lower
left hand, the surrender must be complete, the offering whole-hearted. To the extent that the personal
will exerts its own individual notions in all matters,
particularly spiritual, to that extent will sadhana be
unsuccessful and fraught with obstacles and delays.
To affect a total self-giving of the entire being to the
blessed chosen ideal, a study of Mother Kali's powerful lotus feet of bliss will be helpful.

To begin, it may be asked why the Mother's feet
are symbolized by this rare flower. The lotus grows
with its roots, stalk and stem under water. This
indicates that the Mother's concern and influence
penetrate far below into the depths of the relative
world. On a cosmic level, this represents Her abid-

ance at the very foundation of physical existence where Her most needy children struggle to survive. Spiritually and symbolically, the root, stalk and stem represent the spinal column with its three initial centers. Consciousness in average human beings resides at these three vortexes, called lotuses in the language of the Kundalini Yoga system, and reflects the normal human drives characteristic of relative existence. Thus, it can be said that the Universal Mother has extended Her lotus feet directly into the troubled territory of human problems, planting them there to grant guidance and protection while infusing the domain of life and death with Her transforming primordial power.

The leaves and flowers of the lotus grow above water in the bright sunshine. The leaves are the conductors of wisdom energy, representing stages of spiritual growth that absorb the sunlight of Truth and Knowledge and soak up the Mother's precious teachings that fall like raindrops from celestial regions. When the time is auspicious for spiritual awakening, the young buds of potential realization burst forth as attractive flowers, epitomizing the very essence of illumination. These young flowers represent the opening of the fourth center of consciousness at the heart region. The birth of devotion and spiritual sensitivity spring from this awakening and signal the arrival of all that is good and beneficial in life. This is the first substantial fruit which comes as a result of taking refuge in the Divine Mother of the Universe.

As the young lotus grows and matures, its attracting fragrance spreads upwards to even more sublime regions. The centers at the throat and the forehead open and awaken the power of wisdom transmission and mystical vision. The refuge once sought after amidst the troubles of relative existence has led to the discovery of new territory. From the place of earthly pilgrimage to the rare and remote temple of refined awareness, and from the Mother's wisdom feet of shelter to Her compassionate heart and cosmic mind, the purpose of human existence gets revealed and fulfilled. This journey takes place both physically and spiritually, both literally and symbolically, and the Supreme Being who guides it is intrinsically real. The Upanishads speak of this infinite Supreme Being and reveal the need for taking refuge there:

> Verily, that One is the indwelling Spirit in all.
> Fire is Its head, the sun and moon its two eyes,
> the four quarters of the universe are Its ears,
> the universe is Its heart,
> the revelation of scripture is Its cosmic mind,
> the wind is Its breath, music is Its voice,
> and from Its feet the earth has originated.
> (Mundakopanishad)

At the summit of this auspicious spiritual ascent, the fullest, largest and most eternal lotus abides. This is the center in the crown of the head. With an infinite amount of brilliant petals, this amazing bloom is the comprehensive work of a master gardener. This lotus exudes the intoxicating fragrance of pure love, pure knowledge, pure devotion and pure bliss. Its soil is absolute freedom, its atmosphere indivisible unity, and it basks in the sunlight of nondual Truth. The nectar of immortality drips from it incessantly and liberated souls drink that ambrosia and remain transported in indescribable delight, indefinitely. Of refuges, this is the blessed sanctuary where all pilgrimages cease, for no coming or going is possible where no second place exists! This is the ultimate secret of the Divine Mother's ingenious design. The same healing atmosphere and inseparable nature is present throughout all modes of existence. Her wisdom feet of refuge and Her boundless transcendent mind are one realm, containing and unifying all opposites and extremes, no matter how diverse. With this realization firm in heart and mind, Her children explore the infinite expanse of consciousness, free of fear and prepared for dynamic experience or deep absorption in turns. All this has proceeded from the act of taking refuge in Her lotus feet.

There are three authentic and primary ways through which the blessed Divine Mother's feet of refuge are recognized and accessed — through the *Guru*, through the scriptures, and through the personal desire for liberation. All three are manifest on earth by Her Grace, but all three are difficult to attain and must be earned. There are many *upagurus*, or secondary teachers, inhabiting the physical realm and many pretenders as well, but the authentic guru or spiritual teacher bears the essence of the scriptures in the heart and the ability to transmit them in the mind. What is more, such a teacher already possesses liberation through the Universal Mother's sublime Grace. When the perfect time arrives for receiving this subtle transmission, the aspirant will not have long to wait. Nor will the often fruitless and endless search for the "perfect" guru occupy the time and energies of mature aspirants. The Divine Mother sees and knows all. Her omniscience is impeccable, Her scrutiny complete and constant.

To explain the dynamics involved in the process of taking refuge is practically impossible. With regards to this world and normal human consciousness, the appearance of the guru, the scriptures, and the desire for liberation seems to be a practical and methodical sequence, one coming naturally after the next in succession. In actuality, though, the Divine Mother's intent to awaken human consciousness is predestined. The desire for liberation will always come first according to Her personal transmission, and this will manifest in various ways according to differing temperaments and the conditions inherent in the soul. Though beings may be unaware of it, an inner prompting has already taken place by the time the spiritual preceptor and the precious teachings arrive on the scene.

The Divine Mother's Grace is most subtle, lightning swift, yet manifesting in the most natural of ways. Being One, of the very nature of unified Consciousness, this is Her supreme and unthinkable secret — supreme, since there is no higher or more complete condition, and unthinkable because it defies the mind and its penchant to think and analyze at every turn. The term refuge, then, is a kind of contradiction in terms. Since there is nothing separate from Divine Reality, nothing that is not divine in origin, there is only abidance in Her, only eternal refuge. Even evil and suffering must take their subservient places as Her bond slaves, Her tools for revealing goodness and teaching awareness. This is Mother's powerful nondual Reality, consisting of dynamic energy and static transcendence, and it all takes place at Her lotus feet.

7
Garland of Human Heads

The Ultimate Sacrifice ~
Into the Cosmic Mind-stream

Gracing the Divine Mother's beautiful form and encircling Her lovely neck is an awesome spectacle — a necklace of human heads. The severed head hanging from Mother Kali's hand is a fresh example of this phenomenon, soon to be added to that collection. These were once personalities — individual ego structures that accomplished the transcendence of attachment to name and form and became blissfully absorbed in their chosen ideal.

The garland of heads has considerable significance. First, it symbolizes the transcendence of attachment to earthly life and all its mundane concerns. This is verily accomplished by a gradual and increasing identification with the source of existence which is more peaceful than earth's most serene regions and more attracting than all the enticements that the world has to offer. Secondly, it demonstrates the truth of the unity of all existence in that all races and all beings have one common substratum as their fundamental basis for existence. These two mighty principles, transcendence and unity, combine to create a powerful and comprehensive representation of Truth.

The attempt to transcend suffering based on the vision of unity gives rise to a promise of something higher, more substantial, and ultimately fulfilling.

With it comes the possibility of transcending all earthly concerns, whether they involve detrimental habits and obsessions or mere repetitive cycles of superficial worldly ritual. Bad habits and pressing problems occupy entirely too much of our precious time. Few attain the equipoise and subtle bliss of living life in a spiritual manner. The Universal Mother holds this possibility out to us daily and intends for us to embrace and enjoy this great boon. Realizing the divinity within and expressing it in daily life is a blessing that the Universal Mother bestows upon those who are sincere about refining their awareness. Those who are seriously committed to the methods which the guru and the scriptures recommend reach the highest station of human existence. The members of Her garland of heads represent some of those who have achieved a return to this perfectly natural state.

A circle symbolizes perfection. It also signifies continuity. The Divine Mother's circle of illumined personalities represents the birth, life and dissolution of entire races and cultures from time immemorial. Continual rounds of birth and death resulting in ages (*yugas*) of planetary existence are contained within this powerful symbol, indicating both Her lordship over the universal process and Her absolute mastery over life and death. In fact, the circle of heads, all of serene countenance, reflects in its members the attainment of peace and an absence of fear and worry. Death has been recognized as an illusion, and life as a continual tug of war between

opposing factions which are ever at odds. Those
who have seen through the illusion, attained victory in the war and transcended the enticements of
the play of relativity have arrived at the doorway
leading to the ultimate experience. Consciousness,
arriving at this plateau, becomes subtle and refined
and resembles a playground where bliss flows unin-
hibited. The nightmares of relative existence fade
away swiftly in this internal paradise and divine
remembrance takes its place.

The head — the human mind — is the seat of
the memory and intellect, thus is very important.
All individual minds are microcosmic images of the
universal mind of the Divine Mother. It is She who
acts through all bodies and perceives through every
sense organ. She also analyzes, intuits and remem-
bers through all intellects and memories. The *Katho
Upanishad* explains nicely:

> *That One, the eternal among noneternals,*
> *the intelligence in the intelligent who,*
> *though one, fulfills the desires of the many —*
> *those wise ones who perceive It*
> *as existing within their own Self —*
> *to them belongs peace, and to none else.*

Peace, the vast quietude of ultimate fulfillment and
perfect contentment, attends those minds that dwell
in remembrance of their pure and stainless divine
nature. The smiling faces gracing the Divine
Mother's garland of heads emanate peace and bliss
instead of the horror of decapitation. This reveals

that the illumined mind given to the Universal Mother remains absorbed constantly in deep contemplation of Reality. Other conditions then no longer appeal — not heavenly delights and certainly not the mundane attractions of the world, what to speak of the negativities entertained by the unillumined mind. This is perfect and natural meditation at its best.

Meditation, which is the essence of spiritual life and the crown of attainment in spiritual discipline, is portrayed in fine form amidst the members of the Mother's garland of heads. Distant inward gazes reflect the degree to which each of them has contemplated the cause of their liberation. The Divine Mother has freed them from their constricted sense of individuality, destroying the narrow concerns which once imprisoned them in a world of desires and attachments. She has further bestowed upon them the ability to detach from the world at will and immerse the mind in healthy introspection. In this way, the garland of heads forms the Mother's own army of contemplatives, those in whom the rare gift of subtle perception is developed, allowing them to see through the deluding power of *Mahamaya* and the illusory nature of the universe She has created. Encircling the Universal Mother's lovely form, these radiant minds, absorbed in deep contemplation of the Self in all, enjoy the bliss of inner communion with the source of existence.

Another facet demonstrated by the garland of human heads is the subtle truth of eternal existence.

As Swami Vivekananda states, *"When a clay jar is destroyed, the idea of the clay jar still remains."* Even though the form of a thing may indeed exist no longer, its essence or subtle nature persists as a thought or an idea. If such a thing is true of an insentient object, how much more applicable it is for a sentient being filled with consciousness. Even our bodies, made up of materials that gradually break down and dissolve, continue to exist in subtle form in the minds of our loved ones after we pass on. Since the individual minds of all beings are portions of the cosmic mind of the Universal Mother, and all memories are stored in these microcosmic cells like power in the cells of a battery, the subtle and continual existence of all beings is a permanent fact, even on the physical level. This is only possible and plausible if we accept the essential nature of Consciousness to be timeless, deathless and eternal.

With regards to the Mother's garland of heads, there is a song that states, *"O Mother, where did you get that garland of heads, which must have been in existence long before the universe was born?"*[6] This line holds a deep explanation to the sublime mystery of timeless, deathless awareness. The seed thoughts which form the basis for individual existence are present in subtle form as intelligence even before the universe is formed. The natural conclusion, then, points to the existence of an intelligent creator of the universe who exists before physical manifestation takes place. This in turn implies that matter is the product of intelligence and a tool for its expression. This idea is further understood by the analogy of the inventor. The inventor first conceives of the invention within the mind in thought form. He then proceeds to manifest that idea into the physical realm using the materials at his disposal. On a cosmic level, the Universal Mother does much the same thing. Her infinite intelligence gives birth to all manner of forms which She expresses using the principles of nature as Her materials.

This, then, is the further significance of the garland of human heads. All races and cultures and the many expressions and manifestations which spring from each one of them all pre-exist space and time. This helps us to formulate a definition of eternity that is meaningful and affirmative of life and existence. As vast as it is, it can never be devoid of heart and soul, of intelligence and consciousness, for eternity itself is an idea born of pure Awareness. Whether this timeless, deathless, and causeless Awareness remains static and supine, poised in the breathless stillness of nondual meditation, or decides to enter a sportive mood, eternity is there, ready for expression. This play of Consciousness, the interaction between formless Reality and dynamic energy, is called the *Mahalila,* and the garland of human heads represent so many avenues for its implementation.

8
Her Nakedness

The Exposure of Pure Revelation

The Divine Mother of the Universe, *Kali,* is the essence of all gods and goddesses. She is *Ishvari,* the true Mother of all beings, to whom they turn for all matters pertinent to their needs and desires. She is *Jagadamba,* the presiding deity of the world, and *Tripura Sundari,* the presiding deity of the three worlds. She is the *Mahashakti,* the creator, preserver and destroyer of the universe of name and form. She is also *Mahakala,* one with *Brahman,* completely interchangeable with formless Reality as pure conscious Awareness. In clearly understandable terms, She is Truth.

Truth is irrepressible, victorious, immutable and free of coverings. No limiting adjunct or superimposition can obscure It. It is immediate, predominant and hides nothing, being of the very nature of revelation itself. It is the most corrosive substance in existence, dissolving all barriers, obstacles, veils and layers that would attempt to hide It. Therefore, in essence, It is naked, and completely impossible to cover. As darkness cannot exist around the sun, so also ignorance fails to appear around Truth. Even its polar opposite, falsity, is an idea that does not occur in Its presence. Truth, like other purely positive qualities, defies its antithesis completely and successfully.

In the light of this comprehensive and uncompromising definition of Truth, we can better understand the nature of Mother Kali. Her name means "time." Time is the witness of all phenomena that ultimately and inexorably gets to the very truth of all matters. With characteristic detachment, time perceives the workings of all principles. Her name also implies "space," for another epithet bestowed upon the infinite and supreme Goddess is *Digambari* — "She who wears space as Her only garment." Clothed in nothingness, dressed in the boundless void, even Mother Kali's appearance in the universe of name and form is formless! How inexpressible and incomprehensible, then, must be Her essence beyond the boundaries and impositions of universal manifestation!

Pure revelation, precognitive intuition, immediate perception amidst spontaneous action — these are appellations pertaining to Mother Kali. She is ever present, then, but exquisitely subtle, like the Truth that She so fully epitomizes. Her subtle nature serves to veil the obvious purity of Her presence from extroverted minds. This phenomenon, illusory by nature, is likened to the eye which sees but which cannot see itself. In this way do living beings become oblivious to Her Reality. To rectify this basic error, the minds of living beings must make an intense inner pilgrimage to transcendent Awareness in order to receive Her vision. Whereas other more limited powers of Absolute Reality rule over earthly and celestial regions, granting their votaries boons in accordance with their respective capacities, She is the presiding deity over the realm of formlessness that transmits such stunning attainments as Truth, freedom, unity, fearlessness and the ineffable experience of nondual Awareness. In this way is She the bestower and master of *Nirvikalpa Samadhi*, the state of complete union with Divine Reality.

Goddess Kali is naked — by nature, devoid of any and all superimpositions that may limit or cloud the Truth that She epitomizes. The Truth that She duly represents, teaches and transmits, flows through the conduits of the guru and the scriptures and manifests in the heart and mind as direct spiritual experience *(anubhava)* when the mind is sufficiently purified.

Truth is indeed hard to define. The following "Twenty Truths of Truth," all beginning with the sacred letter, "A," confer a deeper understanding of this great principle. They are *Achintya, Achuta, Adbhuta, Agadha, Agrahya, Akhanda, Akshara, Akshaya, Amala, Anadi-ananta, Anirdeshya, Anugraha, Aparinami, Aparoksha, Aprameya, Apurva, Arupa, Asthula, Avaikalya and Avyaya.*

The Twenty Truths of Truth

Truth is *Achintya,* incomprehensible, because It cannot be grasped by the mind and intellect due to Its nondual essence. The mind and senses depend upon external phenomena to aid in the comprehension of Reality, whereas Truth does not, being the very essence of transcendent Reality. Only a small portion of Its boundless expanse can be apprehended by the mind. This is called knowledge. Truth is eternal, knowledge is Its reflection, depen-

dent upon It. The triad of knowledge, knower and
the act of knowing occurs only in relativity and does
not exist in the unified atmosphere of Truth, for distinction based upon diversity does not occur there.
The quality of Truth called *Achintya* reveals that
Truth is always one and without a second and that
Its expressions occur only from the standpoint of
relativity. It would be easier for the eyes to count
the waves upon the stormy surface of a boundless
ocean then it would be for the ordinary mind to
comprehend the essence of nondual Truth.

Truth is *Achuta,* indestructible, due to Its eternal
nature and Its complete independence from the
realm of name and form where death holds sway.
Death, decay, negativity, inconsistency and imperfection are illusory superimpositions overlaying
Reality. They proceed from the mind's attachment
to relative existence and acceptance of its limiting
adjuncts. Everlasting life, immortality of the Soul,
timeless Awareness — these are things which pre-
vail forever, being the fundamental nature of unified
existence. The truth of these abiding principles is
everlasting and therefore indestructible. The quality
of Truth called *Achuta* reveals death to be an illusion, disease and suffering to be purifying experiences, and Consciousness to be eternal. It would be
far easier to put out the sun's fires with the earth's
oceans than it would be to destroy Truth.

Truth is *Adbhuta,* wonderful, for all negativities,
delusions, inconsistencies and illusions are destroyed
by Its immaculate and all-powerful presence. When
these unwanted impositions are destroyed by the

one-pointed force of nondual Truth, the shining and radiant expanse of limitless spiritual experience becomes revealed and accessible. The awe and wonder at beholding such a vision, participating in it, and absorbing its essence is beyond description. Through *Adbhuta* comes the bliss of Truth which blends the love and devotion of the heart with the purity and perception of the exalted mind, forming them into one beatific expression. The quality of Truth called *Adbhuta* reveals that the source of existence is a perpetually living Reality that radiates knowledge and love. It would be more possible to thread the eye of a needle with a rope than it would be to remove the quality of wonder from Truth.

Truth is *Agadha,* unfathomable, since It contains no limitation and defies all attempts to plumb Its infinite depths. This is, again, due to Its boundless and inseparable nature. As space goes on and on like an endless void yet still maintains a background over which thought and matter can manifest, so Truth remains infinitely expansive while continuing to support all of Its profound yet subtle qualities. It is the nature of Truth to attract and absorb refined intelligence into Its incomprehensible recesses. Since It possesses the power to unify consciousness and make it one with Itself, It is both untraceable and unfathomable. The quality of Truth called *Agadha* reveals that there is no end to the pervasiveness of Reality. To capture, bind or escape from one's shadow would be an easier accomplishment than to plumb the depths of Absolute Truth.

Truth is *Agrahya,* inconceivable. It is not only

unthinkable to the mind and intellect lodged in duality, but It is also inconceivable in Its entirety to Itself since It is Infinite. None can approach Its pristine region without giving up all concepts and suppositions that are born of the mental process and therefore finite. The blazing radiance of realization is Truth's perpetual condition. It is perfectly omniscient yet fully spontaneous. Its emancipated and unified nature place It beyond even the most enlightened understanding. Therefore, It is worshipped and revered by all lovers of Truth. The quality of Truth called *Agrahya* reveals Reality to be boundless and unapproachable for all but those whose minds have become immersed in nondual understanding, having rid themselves of the false and deeply embedded idea that the body and intellect alone constitute ultimate Reality. It would be far more possible for a child to count every grain of sand on earth than for the limited mind to grasp Truth's inconceivable expanse.

Truth is *Akhanda,* indivisible, due to Its homogenous and seamless nature that is impossible to fragment, distill, dilute or separate. Since Its nature is one cohesive essence, the thought or possibility of fragmentation does not occur in It. Even from the standpoint of relative existence, though parts and portions of Truth may appear and disappear with regards to the thinking process and in relation to universal laws, Truth Itself remains integrally one. The quality of Truth called *Akhanda* causes all aspiring minds seeking illumination and freedom from relativity to realize the essential unity of all existence. It would be an easier task to permanently separate an ocean with a carving knife than to cause Truth to divide its cohesive nature. Truth is *Akshara*, imperishable, for Its nature is stainless, pure, undecaying and eternal. In effect, an object or thing can be destroyed and still exist, such as the semblance of a building or the shell of a tree. It is not so with Truth. Destructive elements cannot weaken or corrupt Its character, which is not only impossible to defeat but is also impervious to death. As the Upanishads declare, fire cannot burn It, water cannot wet It and wind cannot dry It up. Neither can antagonistic opponents destroy It or defeat It. This is because It pre-exists the manifestation and appearance of the universe and, in fact, is the very basis for its existence. Though Truth is scarcely recognized, seldom followed and rarely realized, It nevertheless exists in Its own essential nature at all times and under all conditions, despite apparent permutations, obscurations and suppressions imposed upon It. The quality of Truth called *Akshara* provides convincing proof that God alone is Real and the universe is but a reflection of that Reality — that the immortal Soul of humanity is constant and abiding while the body/mind mechanism is transitory. It is more likely that all the suns in the vast heavens be extinguished simultaneously rather than Truth undergo destruction.

Truth is also *Akshaya*, undecaying. An object or thing may remain in existence for an interminable period, yet gradually decay over time. This is not the case with Truth. In this regard, it is not mere longevity that defines Truth, but eternity. Truth is an eternally abiding principle, not a physical element, a vibratory movement or a mental projection. Its existence always remains perfect and without blemish, stain or deterioration. Its very nature is wisdom, freedom and unity, all of which share the same everlasting stability. Truth is ever-fresh, spontaneous, inspiring and fulfilling. The quality of Truth called *Akshaya* allows the mind to transcend doubts, perceive its true nondual nature as limitless Awareness and realize itself to be all-enduring. It would be a far simpler matter to await and behold the dissolution of the universe than it would be to witness the demise of Truth.

Truth is *Amala,* stainless and without impurity. The world of name and form, matter and mentation, contains an abundance of inconsistencies and impurities, for it is only a transitory manifestation or expression of the immutable Reality. The ideals and attainments held sacred by worldly beings abiding in relativity become tarnished and polluted over time and only get discarded for other equally inconsistent replacements. The ideal of Absolute Truth, stable and consonant, captures the faith and devotion of all who would comprehend the essence of Reality, and this is due, in part, to Its sterling nature. The quality of purity has an inherent attraction for minds seeking higher truths, for it is in the purest atmosphere alone that lasting peace and contentment abide. The salient quality of Truth called *Amala* reveals the world of phenomena to be ultimately lacking in satisfaction and demonstrates the superior nature of spiritual qualities and values over the attractions and enticements of relative existence. It would be an easier task to convince all the illumined beings of the seven worlds to trade holy communion for riches, fame and terrestrial power than it would be to tarnish or stain the Eternal Truth.

Truth is *Anadi-ananta,* without beginning or end. It is not only deathless, then, It is also free of birth. The cosmic process and the universal laws which operate it, the coming and going of living creatures in and out of existence, all this falls within the inexorable boundaries of time, which witnesses the manifestation and dissolution of all things. Truth easily escapes the limiting constrictions of time and its accompanying adjuncts such as birth and death because it is anterior to life and mind. Being the most primal and quintessential quality, divine in origin, Truth lives on forever, free of transformations of any kind. The quality of Truth called *Anadi-ananta* proves to living beings that their eternal nature is beyond the limits of time, space, causality and temporality. It would be easier to explore and mark the boundaries of the universe than it would be to rob Truth of Its birthless and deathless condition.

Truth is *Anirdeshya,* completely indescribable. Incomprehensible and inconceivable, Truth is also beyond description. It can be discussed and analyzed only from the standpoint of relativity, for mind and senses, caught in the fundamental trap of delusion with regards to duality, are unable to express nondual essence. As Sri Ramakrishna, the Kali Yuga Avatar, has said, *"Everything has been defiled, as it were, by the tongue of mankind, even the scriptures. The Truth of Brahman, however, can never be defiled, but remains ever-pure."* Since rational explanations fail to express the essence of Truth, it stands to reason that one must go beyond the logical mind and the intellectual process to experience It. Therefore, the quality of Truth called *Anirdeshya* introduces the powerful idea of subtle essence to the minds of aspiring seekers and transmits the knowledge that transcendent Awareness is beyond mere intellectual realization and entirely free from all impositions appearing within the realm of relative existence. It would be far easier to read and explain every book ever written in all languages than it would be to describe the essence of nondual Truth.

Truth is *Anugraha,* Grace. All higher experiences that have ever descended into the minds of human beings have had Truth for their essential ingredient. If Grace is the beneficent boon of the Blessed Lord and Divine Mother of the Universe, then Truth is the pure atmosphere through which that sacred transmission takes place. Only something so incredibly pristine could act as a medium to confer the holy presence and sweet will of the Lord. As a man has rest and security in his home with his family, so the Universal Being has as a foundation the vast support of eternal Truth. Resting forever on this indestructible platform, *Ishvara* executes the decisions affecting the lives of all beings within the seven realms of existence. The quality of Truth called *Anugraha* reveals that God is both with form and beyond form, but is undoubtedly the truth of life and existence. Truth devoid of Grace is as likely as a creation devoid of a Creator. It is more likely that sun and fire fail to radiate heat than that the quality of Truth be bereft of Grace.

Truth is *Aparinami,* changeless, for though it filters down into aspiring intellects as various teachings pertinent to both spiritual wisdom and worldly knowledge, Its nondual essence never varies despite the permutations of external influences. It is not, however, merely static and immovable, but also expresses Its inherent perfection in phenomenal ways. These expressions of Truth permeate the fabric of relative existence and infill it with vibration and animating life-force. Despite an infinite display of awesome variety and expression, the essential nature of Truth remains constant and immutable. The quality of Truth called *Aparinami* reveals both higher wisdom and secondary knowledge to be expressions of one indivisible Reality and demonstrates the subtle principles of unity in diversity and action in inaction. It would be an easier task to count the leaves on every tree on earth during autumn than it would be to witness the slightest change in nondual Truth.

Truth is *Aparoksha,* immediate and direct. This striking quality often manifests at the time of spiritual realization. It is the lightning swift stroke of direct perception inherent in Truth that brings the seer face to face with Absolute Reality. The swift appearance of this powerful force of immediacy is ingrained in everything, whether recognized or not, whether acted upon or not. It lends Truth Its irrepressible ring of undeniable authority and authenticity and causes the universe to radiate with vibrancy. The quality of Truth called *Aparoksha* puts to death all delusion and complacency and reveals the vision of spiritual perception and moment to moment perfection in their place. It would be easier to control multiple flashes of lightning in a thunderstorm by stopping them at their source with one's bare hands than it would be to take the swift and direct spontaneity away from Truth.

Truth is *Aprameya*, immeasurable, for It always remains simultaneously unified and infinite. Truth has unfathomable depths and unforeseeable boundaries. It may appear to expand and contract according to time, place and situation, but since there is nothing outside of Its boundless expanse, this remains only an appearance. Its perpetuity is one of Its most remarkable features which aids in the acquisition of other qualities such as devotion and reverence. The precious quality of Truth called *Aprameya* reveals the futility of ascribing or attributing boundaries to what is infinite. It therefore engenders the quality of acceptance of Absolute Reality in the minds of human beings and expands their inner vision. It would be more possible for a gnat to navigate the infinite expanse of space on its two wings than it would be for the mind to measure the boundless territory of nondual Truth.

Truth is *Apurva*, extraordinary and incomparable, for there is nothing equal to It. Without Truth, none of the divine qualities could exist. It is the essence of all attributes, their best part and quintessential portion. Therefore, It is sought after and valued most highly by all saints and sages of every religious persuasion. Possession of It insures the realization of God. It is the foundation for all other systems of spiritual growth as well as their accompanying disciplines and is the justification for their existence. Without the quality of *Apurva*, habitual preoccupation and mundane human convention become the norm and all higher and more subtle expressions of Truth get masked or obscured. The quality of Truth called *Apurva* allows humanity to perceive the need for higher pursuits and gives them the impetus and thirst for Truth that drives them towards realization of the Self. It would be easier to slake one's burning thirst in the desert by eating sand than it would be for Truth to lose Its extraordinary character.

Truth is *Arupa*, formless, because It epitomizes all that is subtle, unseen and imperceptible in comparison to that which is always associated with name and form. It stands as the eternal principle and the abiding power within everything, yet remains invisible to the senses and even outstrips the mind and intellect. It therefore clearly illustrates the need for transcending the universe and its cosmic laws while simultaneously teaching the lessons of detachment and refinement of consciousness. The quality of Truth called *Arupa* teaches us that, even in this world of name and form, what is imperceptible and unseen forms the substratum for that which is visible and manifest. From this realization comes respect for all life and reverence for the Supreme Being who both utilizes and transcends all limiting ideas regarding form and formlessness. It would prove much easier to capture and contain the entire sky in a wire net than to strip nondual Truth of its formless nature.

Truth is *Asthula,* subtle. It does not get reflected in dark, gross or limited confines, but rather in light-filled and open fields and receptacles. Truth, reflects best in matters directly pertaining to the Spirit. Its primary characteristic, then, is to reveal the supramundane levels of consciousness, which makes it the best barometer for measuring quality and content in all aspects of life, earthly or spiritual. Its subtlety does not rob It in the least of Its exhilarating quality or Its lofty character, but serves to filter out all that is gross and dense. Without the ingredient of *Asthula,* Truth would be exacting but harsh, uncompromising but irrational. The quality of Truth called *Asthula* awakens limited consciousness to higher awareness and confers sensitivity upon it, revealing the internal realm of pure Spirit. It would be far easier to gather up dispersed mustard seeds in a windstorm than it would be to separate Truth from its subtle nature.

Truth is *Avaikalya,* perfect. It is inherently complete, needing nothing, lacking nothing. After contemplating all things desirable, It appears to aspiring beings as the only authentic perfection in the seven realms of existence. Knowledge distorted by misapprehension, can never mar It, neither can wisdom in its highest state of maturation express It fully. The knowledge that there is something in existence that is free from imposition and devoid of imperfection drives seekers of spiritual experience to new heights of insight and realization. *"Through paths of trouble to perfection's goal,"*[7] this is the way of all sincere lovers of Truth. The quality of Truth called *Avaikalya* is the essence of inspiration and aspiration, revealing that the goal of perfection is not a condition that is attainable, but rather an ever-present verity that is the very essence of our true nature. It would be more probable to behold the polar regions without snow and the deserts without sunlight than it would be to comprehend Truth without its essential perfection.

Finally, Truth is *Avyaya*, inexhaustible, for Its strength is all inherent within Itself. Nothing weak or inconsistent can attach to It and no limiting adjunct can adhere to It. This everlasting nature pertains to Its content as well, for endless emanations of Truth are possible, all based in Reality. Truth is so enduring as to outlast infinity, so stable that It persists despite the temporary appearance of the universe over Reality and in spite of the covering of ignorance over the collective minds of beings. The extent of Its pristine power remains untapped even after countless cosmic cycles have come and gone. Its pertinacity is a quality that endears It to all seekers of illumination and all lovers of Truth. The quality of Truth called *Avyaya* confers courage and fearlessness, transforming a weak and tentative nature into a bold and intrepid Spirit. Fear, sense of lack, and insecurity are thereby removed from the mind, leaving it peaceful and serene and in a transcendent and victorious condition. It would be easier for the planets to lose their rotation and the universe to lose its spaciousness than it would be for Truth to lose its inexhaustible power.

Thus, in the rendering of these twenty attributes of Truth, it becomes clear that all of Its qualities are pure, boundless and transcendent. This correlates well with the description of Mother Kali as naked Truth, devoid of even the slightest trace of obscuration. Even in the world of becoming, where the clashing pairs of opposites collide in interminable war, Her nature as Truth radiates constantly without diminishing. As Ramprasad, Her fully committed devotee, sings:

Vigorously She strides
through the battleground of suffering,
Her Tresses of Power flowing wildly!
Who? Who? Who is She?
Her body not protected by a single garment,
She stands fearlessly in the chaos of battle.
She is primordial beauty!
Her cry of Truth sounds forth –
Stop! Stop! Cease and be still!
Her presence eventually enchants
the heart and mind of every being.[8]

9

Her Awesome Appearance

The Spectacle that Nullifies

Mother Kali contains and harmonizes contrasting opposites within Her. Her countenance also reflects this in no uncertain terms. Her startling appearance is intoxicatingly beautiful, yet again She can assume a terrible aspect so frightening that a thousand demons could not compete with it. Her unearthly visage is as unnerving as Her actions, the latter lending an unthinkable dimension of horror of Her wrathful side. As the primordial Mother of the Universe, She will give birth to a baby, suckle it at Her breast and then devour it — all with characteristic detachment. This microcosm example of the cycles of creation, preservation and destruction illustrates Her vast power, for She is the dynamic principle of Absolute Reality. To Her, the universe, and the entire cosmic drama taking place there, as vast as it seems to earthly creatures is, as the saying goes, *as insignificant as the reflection of the moon formed atop a puddle of water gathered in the hoof print of a cow.* This is because She is always cognizant that the universe of name and form is only a reflection of what is real. It is superimposed over Reality like the reflection of a city on the surface of a mirror. She knows that matter and projection are mutable and illusory and that only Consciousness is real and eternal.

Living beings have lost this knowledge and this

fact is the cause of all their suffering. The poet/saint Ramprasad indicates this through one of his wisdom songs: *"Your soul at this moment rests on the gentle lap of Her Cosmic Dream, which you are experiencing falsely as the narrow prison of suffering."* To dispel this illusion, the Universal Mother breaks the habitual patterns of their mundane lives by introducing positive change. This change comes in the form of powerful lessons which involve the destruction of binding habits and constricting limitations. In this way is She known as the Mother who presides over spiritual growth. By breaking down old and antiquated systems of belief and behavior, She keeps the arena of human relations free of stagnation and allows fresh expression and refinement to flow freely. This kind of change is very difficult to accept for beings who have grown used to accepted standards of conventional behavior. For this reason, the Divine Mother presents Her striking and extraordinary appearance. She shocks them out of complacent, habitual and fatalistic frames of mind and this adds impetus to their forward progress.

Her astonishing appearance is associated with cremation grounds. This signifies Her function as guide and overseer of the spiritual progress of human beings. Since most beings are attached to physical existence and take the life of the senses to be the only reality, they suffer at the thought of death and lose faith in the immortal nature of their inner Self. This momentary sojourn on earth comprises a tiny part of a soul's evolution, though an important one. The blessed Mother Kali knows that Consciousness is deathless, birthless and eternal, and while She never tires of teaching humanity the lessons of fearlessness, She simultaneously presides over the function of death, which is a transitional state from one conditional realm to another.

In the symbology of the cremation ground, Mother Kali and Her divine consort, Lord Shiva, represent both the fruition of karma and the force of spiritual emancipation. They reside in the cremation ground, breathing liberating mantras into the souls of those who have attained the lofty status of individual freedom. Ramprasad Sen, the ecstatic devotee of Mother Kali, sings about this subtle phenomenon:

> O mysterious Kali,
> cremation grounds are Your great delight, for
> there You release souls from mundane existence.
> I have transformed my heart
> into a cremation ground
> so You will be attracted here to dance
> in ceaseless, liberating bliss.

The Divine Mother's absolute mastery over death and Her perfect control of its function gets epitomized through this expression. Both the deathless state of liberation and the process of transformation needed to attain that condition are well represented therein. Bold and fortunate are the ones who rise through self-effort to attain *moksha*, the transcendence of suffering and duality culminating in the freedom of the soul.

For those who still remain poised between knowledge of the Self and attraction to the world or karmic bondage, the cremation ground signifies lessons pertinent to the purification process. As detachment and renunciation mature and identification with Reality intensifies, old karmas and residual desires burn away in the fires of self-control, self-surrender and Self-realization. Ramprasad sings joyfully about this process as well:

> O Goddess of Wisdom,
> my limited desires have been consumed
> on the vast pyre of renunciation.
> O Goddess of Freedom,
> I am surrounded by the ashes
> that were my conventional world,
> waiting for You to come.

Thus does the Universal Mother transmit powerful teachings through the destruction of attachment to relativity, thereby causing awareness to focus completely on Divine Reality. The cremation grounds, then, form an important aspect of Her astonishing appearance.

Generally speaking, it is the weak or unawakened that complain of Mother's terrible appearance. Not only these, but the wicked are also put off by Her horrible aspect. Those who are devoted, guilt-free, devoid of evil doings and pure and sincere, find Mother Kali to be both benign and extremely attractive. The poet/saint, Ramprasad, sings about those who have caught a glimpse of Her incomparable beauty by singing, *"No other form can he enjoy."* If Mother Kali frightens the wicked and puts off the ignorant and unawakened, it is only natural that She would attract those who are dedicated, for She is the Mother of all virtues who grants fearlessness and realization. Her unique ability to appear terrifying to some and beautiful to others is due in part to the inherent characteristics and individual capacities of living beings. To realize Truth, one must be courageous and bold, afraid of nothing and willing to encounter all manner of obstacles without faltering. Mother Kali's startling appearance prepares the way for the acquisition of this bold character, as it places challenges in the way to test the mettle of the aspirant who would attain the lofty goal of Self-realization.

What is unknown often terrifies, but overcoming this initial terror builds confidence, strength and the ability to verily surmount all obstacles. Amazingly enough, what terrifies often becomes a source of unending joy and exhilaration. This is true of worldly life as well as spiritual experience. A high dive into a lake or pool, that first ride on a roller coaster, whatever the challenge might be and however much resistance is present at the critical moment, it all gets transformed into joy and confidence by those who persevere and overcome their reticence and fear. For those who fail in these challenges, life not only loses potential for growth and happiness, but begins to become stagnant and lackluster. Such beings compromise their higher ideals and opt for mundane pursuits in an atmosphere of acquiescent safety. This type of person will scarcely venture towards the rigors of spiritual life which demands an open introspection of human nature and many subsequent adjustments.

The minds of those who begin spiritual practices are usually full of negativities and fears. Lasting impressions from previous existences, called *samskaras*, occupy the depths of the subconscious mind like dense swamps or shadowy cobwebs. Activated by undesirable associations and habitual activities, these impressions rise up in conjunction with daily living to create life's hardships and difficulties. Those without a religious orientation or a spiritual path and guide fall prey to these dangerous influences and revert to old tendencies, suffering as a result from negative karma and the many types of bondage that it dictates. Those who meet the problems of internal strife armed with the weapons of self-surrender to God and spiritual discipline, dry up the swamp of detrimental desires and habits and clear the mind of the cobwebs of negative thoughts and intentions. This is the way of purification characteristic of the *Matapatha*, the Mother Path.

Her terrifying aspect, then, is a warning to evil doers, an appearance that separates the strong from the weak and a challenge to compel courageous beings to move swiftly towards the goal of human existence. When the considerable difficulties of life arise and dangers of the mind appear to plague human existence, it is during these times of trial that potential bliss and exhilarating freedom are closest to our grasp, for conflagration, clashing pairs of opposites and extremes attract Mother Kali. In this way, She cleverly causes us to draw our human foibles and hidden imperfections to the surface, bringing us face to face with what ails, frightens and limits us. By confronting our inconsistencies in this way, we learn to destroy our operative karma and neutralize our latent karma, accomplishing in one auspicious lifetime what would ordinarily require many lifetimes to truly facilitate. A vibrant body, a healthy attitude, a clear mind and conscience, and an enterprising spirit are the result of this victory, all beginning with the confrontation of what is dark and fearful within us, symbolized by Mother Kali's awesome appearance.

10

Battlefield of Relativity

Where Opposites Merge

The Divine Mother of the Universe permeates all modes of existence with Her sweet and benign presence. Her formless, homogenous nature pervades physical space as energy, permeates subtle space as thought, and saturates all levels of being as pure, indivisible Consciousness. Her creation, the universe, is replete with many pairs of contrasting opposites, its very fabric being formed of these dualities. Thus, it provides a perfect foundation for active manifestation through the working out of frenetic energies and formulative concepts. In the interim, and while these potential forces and their infinite sets of permutations are interacting with one another, positive and negative effects are constantly arising. Their appearance sets the stage for the continuing clash between good and evil, between life and death, between static and dynamic modes of existence. This field, rife with turmoil and chaos yet possessing the potential for harmony, is the battlefield of relativity upon which the Divine Mother unfolds Her miraculous play of consciousness.

In celestial realms, where gods and goddesses sport, the Mother's power and presence is subtle, manifesting in many wonderful and unimaginable ways. On the cosmic level, the powerful mechanisms of creation, preservation and destruction come into play and the universe is formed. The forceful conflagration involved in this process has been likened to Mother Kali's footfalls. Wherever Her dancing feet encounter a planet, it is destroyed utterly, and whenever an eruption of force manifests anywhere in the universe, it is Her touch that has instigated it. It is on the terrestrial scene, though, on the soil of earth, that the Universal Mother's direct intervention becomes crucially important.

The appearance of the universe is the Divine Mother's doing, since She presides over time, space, causality, life, death and other cosmic functions as *Shakti,* the creative power of *Brahman,* the Absolute. Since She has fashioned this empirical process to be full of contrasting dualities, She must also be present to direct the functions of the laws that She has created so as to control the balance of power. The world is also the field of relative free will where individual beings exert their own personal powers. Virtuous beings, ignorant beings and evil beings all inhabit and share the same planet, some following the natural evolutionary plan and others conspiring against it to use it for selfish and distorted purposes.

The Mother's cosmic plan has unity for its foundation and harmony for its intent. She can brook no alterations to these principles and descends swiftly upon the forces of negativity when any such tampering occurs, bringing Her powerful Will to bear in many ways. For those who are out of step with this plan, She has graciously instilled the process of purification into it. Her cosmic laws and universal forces take care of this for those who are unaware, while an abundance of spiritual methods are available for those who consciously aspire to transcend suffering. In this way, She is the Mother of Souls to those who surrender to Her, the Mother presiding over growth for those who aspire to transcend relativity, and the Mother of justice and retribution to those who follow or disregard Her cosmic laws.

The Mother's Will is inscrutable, Her methods often appearing extreme, unorthodox and even ill-timed to our human understanding. For instance, She may allow evil and negativity its momentary reign of glory in order to accomplish a victorious blow for a higher purpose at a later time. Her omniscience in such matters is infallible. In the meantime, hundreds and thousands march to their deaths in wartime or lose their lives in various catastrophic ways, but it makes little difference. All beings have their lives and deaths in Her, and being one unified field of Consciousness at all times, their individual existences are only temporary conditions, momentary journeys away from their source and point of origin. Even movement and separation are just appearances. As Ramprasad often sings:

"We will be in the end
what we were in the beginning,
bubbles forming and dissolving
in the stream of Mother's timeless Reality."

The lives and deaths of ordinary beings, the bondage and freedom of struggling aspirants, the very idea of ignorance and illumination — all these are only additional sets of contrasting dualities to the Divine Mother who embodies the perpetual state of unified Awareness. Therefore, Her battlefield of relativity serves simultaneously to refine human awareness, demonstrate the need to transcend duality, and confer the revelation of eternal existence. This rendering of the definition of Her divine purpose is broad, logical and based upon the obvious existence of a supreme intelligence existing throughout the universe and beyond. It does not, however, attempt to deal with the unanswerable question of "Why?" One approaches the ocean to frolic on the beach and swim, not to count the grains of sand, categorize the waves or analyze the consistency of the water.

The Divine Mother's battlefield, which constitutes the play of life and death, does not make perfect sense from any rational standpoint. All instruments of analysis at our disposal within relativity are themselves, inherent parts of relative existence. Therefore, all of them, including the senses, mind and intellect, are inadequate to the task of fathoming the Universal Mother's far-reaching intentions for the boundless activity expressing throughout the universe. That all of Her expressions seem to point towards transcendence is the one important key. Therefore, the wise utilize these expressions to acquire this key in order to unlock the treasure chest of nondual understanding.

What they find is the ultimate secret — the truth which reveals that relative existence and transcendence are two frames of reference, both showing a different side of one Reality which, again, permeates them both. The appearance of duality disappears when this realization transforms the mind. The mind then loses its tendency to perceive diversity as being separate from its unified origin. From this vantagepoint there is nothing left to transcend. In this way do the most persistent sets of opposites get dissolved into oneness. This, in part, is true *Advaita Vedanta,* the perennial philosophy, the abiding Truth. Those who live by this verity are hard to distinguish, for as the wise say, *"they have already disappeared while living."* Simplicity mixed with mature wisdom, humility married to strength, a strong adherence to Truth alone — these are a few of the signs of such a supremely illumined status.

It is seen, then, that the world is one with Brahman, not a mirage or an illusion or an unreality. This is true in the ultimate sense, the perfect standpoint, the supreme perspective. Until this subtlest of wisdom is realized and implemented into human awareness, however, the battlefield of relativity serves to bring out and emphasize the lessons pertinent to such a realization. This process is going on at all times, while beings embroiled in the fray act without the least knowledge that every occurrence is fraught with significance and dictated by the supreme will of the Universal Mother. When the warring factions become too intense, Her power, inherent in us as the witness of phenomena, takes over and we draw back to catch a glimpse of that which causes us to detach from the battle, like a veteran warrior retiring to the top of a nearby hill to watch the outcome. If what is witnessed is still of interest, we re-enter the conflagration, perhaps with more knowledge and insight, until finally there is nothing left to bind our attention to the ephemeral world and we open the lock of transcendence.

This signals a new era in the evolution of the transmigrating soul, for never again will the fleeting aspects of the world of name and form hold the same attraction. Some beings will dissolve into their formless essence. Others will return to the play of consciousness, acting without attachment, helping others without selfish motive and working without anticipation for any particular outcome. Whatever the result, the battlefield of relativity plays a vital role in the schooling of souls, and the Warrioress who rages there, adamant yet detached, appears as every teacher and every teaching.

11

Waistband of Human Arms

The Epitome of Perfection in Works

The extensive play of consciousness which takes place on all quadrants of the battlefield of relativity has many participants. Celestial powers associated with the implementation of cosmic laws, divine helpers assisting in the process of refining consciousness, struggling souls attempting to rise out of suffering and misery, naive and ordinary beings unconsciously undergoing a gradual transformation of individual awareness and even rebellious egos plotting to undermine all attempts to bring benefit and goodness into a troubled world — all are vehicles for the sporting of consciousness. The Divine Mother of the Universe, under whose inscrutable guidance all occurrences take place, controls and manipulates them all, wearing their limited powers as an ornament of human arms about Her lovely waist.

The arm and hand are fitting symbols of power and efficiency. Tasks and duties necessary for the maintenance and survival of the human species get accomplished by these instruments. It is fitting that the Universal Mother uses these symbols to indicate that all activities performed throughout the universe are perpetrated by Her power alone. This is true of activities on the vital, mental and spiritual levels as well. Indeed, it is She who unleashes the animating force which flows through the nerves as *prana,* causing the appendages of a host of beings to perform their functions. The individual minds of human beings, which are extensions of Her cosmic mind, transmit subtle thought impulses to the nervous system. Her own detached Consciousness, as the witness of all phenomena, oversees every aspect of this complicated process and maintains the forces that operate the laws of cause and effect which spring from it as well. She is the superior worker, detached yet compassionate, transcendent yet involved. She is the ultimate inspiration and impetus behind every action.

The waistband of human arms represents every type of worker in the Mother's vast army of helpers. Even negative forces work for Her, though they are not aware of this fact. In this way She gets Her work accomplished according to Her own sweet Will. It is interesting to note how single arms adorn Her circle of appendages. This signifies that all who gather around the Universal Mother join in a unified effort for a great cause, and this undertaking is assured of success. The purposes of diverse humanity, most always at odds, are thereby turned towards a common goal and are directed in a harmonious fashion towards an ultimate good. The single arms also designate focus and concentration in work. In much the same way that *"thine eye must be single"* in order to see God, one's work must be accomplished with single-minded purpose to achieve the best result. Work must reflect strength, fortitude and positivity in execution, foresight, knowledge and experience with regards to direction, and care and scrutiny to insure quality. The essential ingredient of detachment from the final outcome is also crucial.

This opens up another dimension of meaning pertaining to the waistband of arms. In this regard, Mother Kali wears them not only to show that She is the agent of all action, but also to indicate the efficacy and wisdom of giving up all attachment to work. These twenty-four aspects of Mother Kali all represent different elements of Yoga. For example, Her wisdom eye represents *Jnana Yoga,* Her crown, as will be seen, indicates *Raja Yoga,* and the Varada Mudra speaks to us of *Bhakti Yoga.* The waistband of arms, then, perfectly epitomizes *Karma Yoga* and transmits the message of selfless works for the good of others. This effective reminder, stark and awesome when first encountered, is Mother's way of telling humanity that work done for the sake of personal motive is binding, whereas action undertaken in Her for the good of others is conducive of higher attainment leading to freedom.

This realm of karma, where acts, thoughts and deeds, whether evil or good, combine with universal laws and cosmic principles to create a residue of powerful effects, is a most difficult area of human life. In part, it constitutes life, for without karma, cause and effect, there would be no universe, no mind, no living beings. Mother Kali illustrates this boldly as She strides across the battlefield of relativity, severing heads and limbs from necks and bodies. In this, Her most favorite occupation, She is essentially capturing minds and plunging them into nondual meditation, collecting the virile energies from active beings and merging them in Her. She thereby transforms the conflagration of war into silent repose. This is the "*Peace, Peace, Peace,*" of the Upanishads, the blissful equipoise desired most intensely, either consciously or unconsciously, by all living beings.

It is through divine Mother Kali, the *Deva Devi Svarupaya,* the combined essence of all powers in the universe and beyond, that beings finally perceive the intrinsic connection between fulfillment and work, experiencing the ultimate unification of action and inaction. In Her exist the synthesis of Jnana, Bhakti and Karma (wisdom, devotion and works) resulting in the highest meditation leading to *Samadhi,* the crowning achievement of Raja Yoga. This is also the profound message of Sri Krishna, delivered most sublimely in the *Bhagavad Gita.* Indeed, the composer of this celestial song and the Wisdom Mother are intrinsically and inseparably related. She is He and He is She; Brahman and Shakti are one. The dark blue Krishna is the black Kali, one and the same. The poet/sage Ramprasad had similar realizations:

> *The One who dances as Divine Love incarnate,*
> *Lord Krishna of the tender heart,*
> *is the very One who rages blissfully as Kali,*
> *consuming names and forms entirely.*
> *Meditate on His Flute and Her Sword as One!*[9]

This lofty truth, wherein gets merged the contrasting ideas of work and worship, thinking and being, is the ultimate secret revealed by the Universal Mother's waistband of appendages. In a sense, this is Her only clothing, the vestige of covering symbolizing work and its cessation which hides Her unthinkable secret of the unity of all existence. Creation, preservation and destruction — birth, life and death — these considerable forces constitute an external play so vast and perplexing, so attracting and enchanting, that beings forget entirely the subtle truth of their eternal nature. Work draws them out, and because of emergence from that internal perfection, the universe of name and form appears before consciousness with all its intrigues and dangers, contentments and insecurities, victories and successes. For this reason does the Universal Mother appear to us with a sword, with a garland of heads, with bracelets of snakes and a waistband of human arms and other striking articles. She will draw us back, take us inward to our source again, convince us once more of our divine nature and plunge us gratefully and irretrievably into the blissful blackness of formless and ineffable peace. There, we will be one with Her and with each other, a conditionless state of inexpressible fullness existing eternally yet impregnating every moment with divine presence. It is no wonder, then, that all minds and energies seek immersion in Her and find ultimate fulfillment there.

12

The Blood of Sacrifice

The Red Tide of Unimaginable Compassion

The poet/sage, Ramprasad, speaks of an enchanting and unforgettable spiritual experience. He sings:

> *Who is this extraordinary feminine presence,*
> *dancing in the universal field of battle?*
> *Truly naked, eternally sixteen,*
> *with magnificent dignity*
> *She stands on the Breast of Absolute Reality*
> *that assumes the aspect of Lord Shiva,*
> *His body also naked in Truth*
> *as He sleeps in supernal contemplation.*
> *All the blood ever shed in sacrifice or conflict*
> *streams down Her brilliant black Form*
> *as crimson flowers float on dark waters...*[10]

This awesome vision of the Black Goddess confers palpable wisdom upon its recipient, and exposes some powerful truths for contemplation as well. One of them, the streams of the blood of sacrifice and conflict, presents us with a very perplexing and possibly incomprehensible dilemma: that of the problem of suffering.

It has been stated earlier that the body, mind, senses and intellect are unable to give us any ultimately satisfying realization of the nondual condition, since they are elements of duality itself, formed from the relative world of evolving principles. Since they have their existence within relativity, they are helpless to solve the problems of relativity which can only be effected by detachment and transcendence. The same problem occurs with regards to the problem of suffering. It is a product of life in relativity and persists as long as the body/mind complex exists. It disappears only in an unconscious state or a transcendent condition. The difference here is that it returns upon awakening from an unconscious state, whereas transcendence either transforms it or puts an end to it.

Suffering is an enigma that even perplexes the minds of illumined beings. Learning its secret, they either default to a higher perspective or resort to a benign refuge. This behavior, characteristic of the wise, indicates the way out of suffering and the ultimate solution of freedom from it. In this regard, Sri Ramakrishna declared, *"You have come to the orchard to eat the mangoes, will you instead spend all your time counting the leaves?"* This sage counsel gives us a key to the problem of pervasive misery. Knowing it to be a fact of physical existence, we can then accept its presence in daily life and begin to shift our focus away from it. This movement allows the mind to develop a subtle ability to bear with trials and troubles while maintaining concentration on matters essential to spiritual growth. In Sanskrit this is called *titiksha,* forbearance. When, through spiritual disciplines, this art of self-mastery has matured, the aspirant has a tool for limiting, dispelling and transcending suffering forever. This comes about in a unique way characteristic of the Divine Mother path.

Using the assertion *"All that exists art Thou"* as the ultimate credo, and taking this to mean that there is nothing outside of Divine Reality, the aspirant begins to understand transcendence, not in terms of escape, but rather in terms of harmonization leading to unity. It is in this way that suffering gets its initial transformation. At the beginning of spiritual life, one is struck by the fact that suffering and those experiences associated with it are the best mediums for bringing about growth. It is also noticed that pleasure and the relative happiness that it brings, more often than not, causes stagnation and the return of misery. This contrast adds weight to these realizations and prompts the mind to ponder the nature of both relativity and Reality. As a result, and over time, the mind begins to accept the ignoble lashes of pain dealt out by nature and karma, building up a healthy tolerance. When this quality of tolerance *(titiksha)* is blended with spiritual guidance in the form of prescribed disciplines coming from the guru and the scriptures, a remarkable occurrence takes place.

The second stroke of transformation on the problem of suffering occurs when *"All that exists art Thou"* begins to pertain directly to one's negative experiences. To actually perceive the Mother's benign hand in all sufferings and punishments clarifies the mind, diminishing its tendency to shirk from what is often a natural outcome of activity in the world. As a result, the aspirant turns upon the oncoming negative experiences, boldly faces them, and welcomes them as messages from the Beloved Lord, remaining both equanimous to the result and conscious of the cause. Courage is born from this aggressive step, a quality which quickly develops an intrepid and enterprising spirit. This phenomenon is clearly stated in Swami Vivekananda's poem, *Kali the Mother: "He who misery loves and hugs the form of death, to him the Mother comes."*[11] Thus does the transformation of suffering, of limitation and of human nature, take place simultaneously, giving birth to the early stages of the realization that God exists in everything, and everywhere.

When the Divine Mother arrives, permeating consciousness with profound insights, the death knell of suffering is sounded once and for all. It is at this juncture of spiritual life, as Vivekananda implies, that work becomes worship, laboring becomes a form of prayer and life itself becomes religion. The unity of all existence, so often spoken of in sacred scripture by the wise, now finally begins to make sense. The triumph over suffering through a deeper understanding of the true meaning of transcendence strips away the final veils from the truth of nonduality, the most precious secret, and reveals the keeper of the secret — the Divine Mother of the Universe. Thus, when this indescribable experience lights human awareness, one begins to truly understand both the purpose and the nature of suffering.

The amazing process of spiritual awakening is a blend of mystical and practical elements. It is the Universal Mother that provides the materials of nature, while living beings either create the web of deception leading to suffering or tread the path of goodness leading to emancipation. It is She, again, who awakens beings to impending danger and provides the impetus which propels them out of their various predicaments and dilemmas. It is this realization, coming into fruition in conjunction with the development of forbearance and success in spiritual endeavors, that impels the mind beyond the idea of suffering. Therefore, it is the Mother's Grace combined with self-effort that hastens the transforming stroke of the wisdom sword of nonduality which falls across the neck of attachment, desire, fear, doubt and complacency. Recognition of the Divine Mother's perpetual presence, taking refuge in Her Grace and surrendering to Her Will, all facilitated through one's personal self-effort — this is the royal road to Self-realization.

For those extremely fortunate ones who combine Grace with perpetual self-effort, a sobering glimpse of Truth appears. It is sobering because so many if not all of the preconceived notions harbored in the mind are exploded and sunk in the fathomless waters of nondual Awareness by this glimpse of Reality. Whereas there is a price to pay for such unobstructed views of pure Reality — the process of awakening being uncomfortable at times — it is nothing compared to the pain caused by ignorance. The repercussions proceeding from acts of detachment from the realm of selfish desires and binding attachments are nullified to a great extent by spiritual disciplines and the helping hand of the Divine Mother, but those without the purifying practice of sadhana pay dearly. They suffer in ignorance without that advance knowledge that spiritual self-effort brings. Sadhana, spiritual practice, is actually faith in action. Both kinds of sacrifice, though — the renunciation of worldly life to attain what is eternal, and the giving up of the kingdom of heaven in order to enjoy the world — are ultimately absorbed by the Universal Mother. She bears the effects of both individual karma and personal transcendence of the world of name and form. Therefore, She is the granter of precious boons to aspiring devotees and the savior of the fallen and lowly as well. The effects proceeding from these two very different kinds of orientations appear as streams of blood which flow down Her radiant black body *"like crimson flowers floating on dark waters."*

It has been declared that the Divine Mother is the totality of Consciousness, providing all the materials of nature and the elements of body, mind and senses through which to experience this amazing universe. Knowing Her to be the door through which the devotees gain access to nondual Reality, reveals Her to be the supreme force behind the universe as well. In addition, She is described by the scriptures as the ground and foundation of all existence, the formless essence over which the universe gets projected. In this totality, an inclusiveness so complete that words such as distinction, division and separation lose their meanings, the streams of blood, denoting suffering at the utmost level of sacrifice, are more easily appreciated.

When a baby is born, suffering the agonies of birth, it is the Mother that wipes the memory of such misery out of the young mind. When a man or woman enters the world of contrasting opposites, bearing its ferocious attacks in various ways, it is the Universal Mother that absorbs these forces and confers the strength and will power to go on. When the world rocks from war, plagues, famines and other catastrophes, the Mother is present, for She is the torn earth, the rent flesh, the anguished mind and tortured spirit of every living being ever to undergo such trials. Finally, when the universe disappears into the final dissolution at the end of a cosmic cycle, it is the Divine Mother of the Universe, the Mother of all souls, that gathers them into Her blissful embrace and protects them from destruction, granting them knowledge of their true nature.

As the mother bears with the pains of childbirth and the slow growth of the infant, as an artist accepts the imperfections and importunities of the creative process, as the contemplative patiently abides with the rebellious nature of the unsteady and restless mind, so too does the Universal Mother willingly accept the lashes of the effects of relative existence upon Her august person. The entire phenomenal process, from manifestation through dissolution, as bittersweet as it seems and as inexplicable as it is, is ultimately justifiable. The spectacle of universal suffering is strangely compelling, the vision of the Mother's sacrifice is eternally inspiring, and the eventual transcendence of pervasive suffering signals the attainment of the goal for human birth. Through the Mother's Grace, such visions bring about an exalted state of mind leading to complete immersion in Divine Reality. This would be impossible without the Universal Mother's ongoing sacrifice, the effects of which appear on Her radiant dark skin in crimson streams.

Another important lesson gets transmitted by this enigmatic symbol — the necessity for the development of sensitivity, both on material and spiritual levels. Creating this mindful state amounts to the practice of moment to moment reverence for all life, even for insentient things. This has been called the deification of the world, for it is in the world, with its substantial dose of illusory influences, that beings lose the perception of their inherent spiritual nature, mistaking momentary experiences and material possessions for Reality. If the earth is seen as Mother, the sky as Mother, the objects encountered by the senses as Mother, the mind and its thoughts as reflective of nothing but Mother, then the streams of blood, representing both physical and mental suffering, will cease to flow so profusely. At that time, the Warrior Goddess will transform into the image and embodiment of Love and existence will be stripped of its painful and perplexing inconsistencies. The experience of nondual Reality will then become a moment to moment condition of remembrance and abidance once again.

13

Mother Kali's Protruding Tongue

The Consumption of the Dual Universe

Gazing upon the awesome visage of the Divine Mother Kali, one encounters an unusual sight. The spectacle of Kali's long, protruding tongue strikes one with wonder, causing questions to arise in the mind. What is the symbolism behind this appearance? Why does Mother Kali so blatantly display Herself in this manner? The meaning, or meanings, are not hard to find and are, as is usual with the Universal Mother, rife with significance.

It has been suggested by some that Goddess Kali, in the fashion of the customary Hindu wife, is extending Her tongue out of shame at having touched with Her feet the body of Her husband, Lord Shiva, who lies beneath Her. Such a thing can be termed as disrespectful when viewed from a cultural context. This interpretation, however, if examined, is seen to be not only unsatisfactory but also illogical. In the first place, Goddess Kali is certainly not a shy bride. She is the Mother of the Universe. Furthermore, Her nature is hardly meek and retiring, but is instead powerful, bold and forthcoming. She has not accidentally brushed against Her lordly husband's body, She has emerged from His innermost heart and is dancing boldly and uninhibitedly over the boundless expanse of formless Reality which He represents. He is pure Consciousness in Its static condition, She is the same Timeless

Awareness in a dynamic mode of expression. He is Shiva, the Lord of gods, She is Shakti, His intrinsic power. He is the *Nitya,* the formless and ecstatic essence of Consciousness, and She is the *Lila,* Its joyful and playful expression. He is the flower, She, the fragrance emanating from it. With these facts taken into account, it is necessary to search elsewhere for the inner meaning of Mother Kali's protruding tongue.

The most substantial representation with regards to this phenomenon is found, not surprisingly, in the sacred scriptures. The *Devi Mahatmyam* and the *Srimad Devi Bhagavatam* both contain references to the famous battle between the horrible demon Raktabija and the Divine Mother, Durga. It is said that this particular battle raged on and on for hundreds of years, each side unable to completely subdue and defeat the other. In this ancient and critical battle between evil and good, between selfish ego-oriented individuality and selfless transcendent Awareness, Sri Durga applied Her most miraculous powers of concentration to defeat this horrible *asura.* Earlier, Raktabija had received a boon from Shiva that conferred upon him the ability to create others like him from each drop of blood that fell from his wounds. Since every drop of blood shed in battle turned into another Raktabija, he presented a considerable problem to his frustrated opponents. Only Mother Durga had the ingenuity to overcome and destroy him. From Her wisdom eye She gave birth to Kali, who sprang as a divine emanation of

indestructible power from Sri Durga's highest meditation.   This powerful *Matrika* was pitted against
Raktabija with disastrous results:

> *Seeing the multitude of asuras marching*
> *against Her, Ambika (Sri Durga) got very angry.*
> *Her eyebrows became crooked, Her face became*
> *black, and Her eyes turned red like Kadali flowers;*
> *at this time suddenly came out of Her forehead*
> *Kali! Wearing a Tiger's skin, cruel, covering Her*
> *body with an elephant's skin, wearing a garland*
> *of skulls, terrible, with a belly like a dried up*
> *well, mouth open, with a wide waist, lip hanging*
> *loosely, with ax, noose, Siva's weapon in Her*
> *hands, She looked very terrible like the night of*
> *dissolution. She began to lick with her tongue*
> *frequently and forcibly dashed into the asura*
> *army and began to destroy it. She angrily began*
> *to take the powerful demons in Her arms and*
> *pouring them into Her mouth crushed them with*
> *Her teeth. Taking the elephants with bells by Her*
> *own power in Her hands She put them all into*
> *Her mouth and swallowed them all with their*
> *riders and began to laugh hoarsely.*

At this point in the memorable battle, Raktabija
enters the fray in order to destroy the supreme
Goddesses. The great sage and writer Vyasa, witnessing the age-old battle, gives us this account:

> *Please hear attentively about the extraordinary*
> *boon that was given by Mahadeva to the great*
> *warrior Raktabija. Whenever a drop of blood from*

the body of that great warrior will drop on the surface of the earth, immediately will arise innumerable asuras, equal in form and power to him. Thus elated with this boon, he entered into the battlefield with great force in order to kill Kalika and Ambika Devi. Seeing the lotus-eyed shakti, the demon struck Her with a violent weapon. She baffled the weapon with Her club and hurled the discus on the great asura. Thus struck by the disc, blood began to ooze out from his body as the red stream of the soft red sandstone comes out from a mountain top. Wherever on the surface of the earth drops of blood fell from his body, then and there sprang out thousands and thousands of demons like him. Indrani, the wife of Indra, became very angry and struck the demon with Her thunderbolt. Many demons instantaneously were born from the drops of blood, having similar weapons and hard to be conquered in battle.

Along with Vaishnavi and Indrani, other Matrikas (emanations of the Divine Mother of the Universe) all attacked Raktabija and struck or pierced him with their weapons. Thus torrents of blood flowed out of his body and thousands of asuras like him were born, covering the battlefield. As the other Matrikas retired from the field, the focal point of the battle then centered around Durga and Kali. At this point, Vyasa records the following conversation between the two Goddesses:

Ambika Devi said to the lotus-eyed Kali, 'O Chamunda! Open your mouth quickly, and no sooner than I strike Raktabija with weapons, you should drink off the blood as fast as it drains out of his body. O large-eyed one! You will drink all the jets of blood in such a way that not a drop of it escapes and falls to the ground. Thus will they be extirpated, otherwise they will never be destroyed.' Chamunda Devi, of ferocious strength, hearing thus the Devi's words began to drink the jets of blood coming from Raktabija's wounds, lapping them up with Her tongue. Thus all the asuras that were created out of the drops of blood were destroyed, and when lastly there was only the real Raktabija left, Ambika Devi cut him to pieces with Her sword and thus exterminated him.

In this account, a more clear and fitting meaning for Mother Kali's prodigious tongue is introduced. She has managed to absorb every drop of blood on the entire battlefield, particularly the blood of the demons that opposed the forces of righteousness. Essentially, She has accepted into Herself all the negativity of the universe, neutralizing it effectively and leaving the field of existence free from danger and chaos. Whereas the streaks of blood emitting from Her own body represent the very principle of sacrifice, Her tongue acts as the tool for its accomplishment and demonstrates Her willingness to come to the aid of all that suffer from misery and oppression. When seen in this light, though the sight of Goddess Kali's tongue may bring discomfort or aversion to the minds of the naive, a deeper understanding of its significance allows for a genuine appreciation and gratitude. In much the same way that the blood of Christ is seen as His sacrifice for the good of all living beings, a form of vicarious atonement in Christianity, in like manner do the streams of blood and the protruding tongue reflect this principle in Tantricism.

Exploring this approach further, it can be said that the Divine Mother of the Universe not only accepts and transforms the suffering of all beings caused by the effects of their karma, She also absorbs and dissolves all phenomena appearing in the universe. Her tongue, then, represents the thirst for life, Her zest for the creative process and the rising and falling of all such urges in the collective minds of Her creatures. The ultimate satisfaction of desires culminating in liberation from attachment to the senses is also implied, for name and form and all associations involved in them get dissolved through Her power, as a cube of sugar dissolves on the tongue.

Finally, comes the perception that the Divine Mother is the very life-force of the universe, symbolized by blood, the essential liquid of sentient life. This is why She is often seen holding the chalice of blood, or skullcup. She drinks the liquid of life to signify that all beings have their existence in Her, and achieve their final immersion in Her as well, all due to Her Grace. Thus is the protruding tongue of the Goddess viewed with awe and appreciation through the eyes of the scriptures and through those wise and fortunate ones who understand the profound significance of sacrifice and transcendence.

14

Lightning Flashes
From Her Teeth

Insights from the Mouth of the Universal Mother

Both the thunderbolt and the lightning flashes associated with Mother Kali have profound significance. The thunder signals the approach of Her wisdom and the lightning heralds the flash of realization proceeding from its revelation. Ramprasad sings about this "electrifying" occurrence:

> *A radiant black storm cloud*
> *expands across the sky of awareness.*
> *The peacock of my mind*
> *reveals its brilliant colors,*
> *dancing with the bliss of holy expectation.*
> *Kali's Wisdom Thunder rumbles profoundly*
> *with Her power that can level mountains.*
> *The fiery tracery of lightning flashes*
> *forms Her Smile of Ecstasy.*[12]

The smile of Goddess Kali is unique and breathtaking, representing a vision so lofty that it is beyond the capacity for even advanced aspirants to perceive. Fully illumined beings encounter such an amazing phenomenon only rarely. As the poet/saint often sings, *"Even sages cannot glimpse Her Form in their daily meditation — only during rare states of total absorption."*[13] This wondrous smile of ecstasy, which exposes the gleaming white teeth of the

Supreme Goddess that devour ignorance hungrily, captivates the souls of all lovers of Truth. Her smile enchantingly blends equal parts of Purity, Truth and Ecstasy into radiant bursts of transcendent insight that enlighten the minds of all those who would gaze upon Reality.

All sense of individuality takes flight during such intense experiences and the human mind becomes so transparent that it disappears entirely. Sri Ramakrishna describes this process:

> God is directly perceived by the mind, but not by this ordinary mind. It is the pure mind that perceives God, and at that time this ordinary mind does not function. A mind that has the slightest trace of attachment to the world cannot be called pure. When all the impurities of the mind have been removed, you may call that mind Pure Mind or Pure Atman. (Gospel of Sri Ramakrishna)

With these words, a sense of the term *Nirvana* is gained. The ordinary mind is simply nonfunctional at such times, and no sense of individual awareness remains. This is the end of mundane existence and the revelation of its transitory nature. It is no wonder that the poet/saint sings, *"None will survive the fury of Her illumination!"*

Given the subtle process of spiritual insight and considering the enigmatic nature of Goddess Kali, it is very difficult to describe or discuss such a profound symbolism. To comprehend what these flashes of insight truly represent, it is necessary to experience them for oneself. This can occur only through the combination of spiritual self-effort and the Divine Mother's Grace, both being rare manifestations. Nevertheless, understanding can also proceed on an intellectual and intuitive level by contemplating the Divine Mother Herself and sincerely yearning for Her vision with one's entire heart. In the process of practicing disciplines, devotions and selfless service for the good of others, the Mother gets attracted and bestows upon Her devotee the first rumbles of inner wisdom. When enough of these powerful thoughts and insights connect and coalesce, like clouds rubbing together in the elevated atmosphere of higher intelligence, radiant explosions of direct perception take place. These flashes reveal the terrain of pure Awareness, allowing glimpses of nondual Truth. From these glimpses are gleaned the kernels of realization which eventually, at the auspicious moment of spiritual evolution, combine to produce full enlightenment called *Samadhi*. This experience is, indeed, *"Her smile of ecstasy."*

It is asserted by all true knowers of Brahman that enlightenment happens by the Grace of a higher will, something beyond the small powers possessed of the human condition. Given that this is true and accepting the unanimous declaration of saints and sages from all religious traditions on the matter, it is wise to consciously take refuge in that Supreme Being. It is She who decides to unveil Her lovely smile, to gnash Her teeth together so as to destroy ignorance and reveal the pure light of Truth. Knowing this, would it be wise to depend upon the individual will and ego and disregard the Divine Will? Would one use a match to light a dark cave when a torch is available? As the scriptures and luminaries never tire of stating, the radiance of a million suns cannot outshine Her, nor can the combined glow from a million moons equal Her beauty. Hers is an unearthly and otherworldly type of loveliness — matchless, incomparable and inexpressible — and only the flashes of nondual insight proceeding from Her Grace can bestow a glimpse of that ultimate vision.

15

Crescent Moon On Her Brow

The Perfect Timepiece: Timing that
Transcends Time

The Divine Mother's Grace grants knowledge, lights and animates the universe, and auspiciously unveils Her own presence at the perfect moment. In the context of human evolution, this is a crucial and all-important matter, for not only does the experience of ultimate peace and bliss proceed from this precious moment, but suffering and misery of all types also come to an end. Mother Kali's most enchanting face and head are often seen graced by the glow of a crescent moon, Her countenance softly lit by its subtle radiance. The moon, with its gradual cycles, epitomizes more than any other object the principle of meticulous timing. How fitting it is, then, that the Divine Mother takes it as Her emblem in order to communicate to aspiring humanity that growth and maturation all happen in a predestined fashion and in accordance with Her supreme will and omniscience.

This symbol is extremely useful, not only as a reminder that patience and perseverance are virtues, but also to help strengthen our resolve by revealing that our divine nature abides within, awaiting discovery. Both of these ways, remembrance and affirmation, play an important part in the process of Self-discovery leading to realization. The crescent moon first acts as a reminder to indicate the movement of cycles in all that we do. Mother Kali's prime concern is in the area of spiritual growth, especially those cycles of growth affecting spiritual awareness. At first, the mind is unaware that it can control emotions and mood swings. Through the timely instructions of an enlightened teacher and an active engagement in spiritual disciplines, a subtle inner strength develops. As the mind becomes stronger and more perceptive due to the practice of prescribed spiritual disciplines, it is easily able to recognize the different movements of energy in its vacillating cycles and identify the characteristics in each. This makes it easier to bear with the low swings of the cycles while fully utilizing their ascents and peaks.

The ebb and flow of energy within any given cycle is very interesting to watch. The sum total of many cycles occurring over time represents a crucial part of spiritual evolution. In time, the aspirant is able to equate the fluctuation of energy within cyclic patterns with Grace, experiencing the coming and going of this subtle principle. At the outset, when awareness is still unrefined, the practitioner must persevere and bear with the mind's periods of restlessness and laziness which come in turns. This set of extremes causes the mind to eventually seek balance and equanimity. Even as consciousness becomes more refined and the mind is partially controlled, the influence of contrasting opposites is still experienced, manifesting as alternate experiences of uncontrollable bliss and unbearable despondency.

It is only when the mind's movements are well known, categorized and controlled, that the fortunate aspirant experiences a release from these extremes and abides in subtle peace. At this juncture, Witness Consciousness has matured in the devotee, allowing for a strong detachment and disassociation from the cyclic rounds of relative existence.

Mother Kali is seen sporting a new moon, a crescent, or a full moon, at different times. Through this symbolism She conveys to us the importance and necessity of recognizing, bearing with, utilizing and detaching from all movements within time. Her name, Kali, refers to time. *Kala* is the Sanskrit word for time, and time is the witness of all phenomena. If the devotee identifies with Kali,the ever-blissful controller of time, the mind's transcendence of all occurrences in space and time is achieved. Through the continual practice of patience and detachment, whether the mind be active or lethargic, the possibility of transcendence becomes real and tangible, finally maturing as steadfast equanimity under all conditions. This is a state of mind much coveted by all seekers of Truth. Through it one enjoys peace and subtle bliss and is always balanced in equipoise.

It is interesting to note that the crescent moon and its waxing and waning cycles are closely related to the three *gunas* often propounded by Vedanta philosophy. *Sattvas,* subtle balance, *rajas,* frenetic activity, and *tamas,* inertia, are three modes of existence which fluctuate constantly, subjecting the minds of living beings to a hypnotic condition. The inertia of tamas must be overcome by activity. When the mental state is lethargic and unable to motivate, a strong dose of will power must be called forth in order to break that slothful condition. This strength must come from within each individual, for relying upon outer stimuli, whether it be from external objects, substances or the aid of other living beings, will offer only momentary solutions. Lethargy will return again and be more impervious to such assistance and harder to cope with the second time. As the mind gets used to the idea that strength comes from within the Self, the patterns of inertia are broken and activity becomes easy to maintain.

As action takes the place of lethargy, the energy of the mind shifts to accommodate a faster pace. The mind then develops a dependence on activity, as if it were a substance that induces euphoric states. In this condition, people often become automatons, driven by the need to accomplish tasks undertaken for personal gain. This is the predominance of rajas, a mode of frenetic activity that thrives in the atmosphere of selfish motivation. The light side of this guna propels one towards satiation, while the darker side binds living beings into avenues of cyclic repetition devoid of any higher attainment. The thought of peaceful liberation from tiresome rounds of pleasure and pain never occurs to beings caught in this frantic maze. Monotony mixed with depletion of vital energy is the result of this type of existence.

It is only through the fulfillment of desires and a longing for release, that an all-important spiritual awakening takes place. This is the appearance of subtle awareness, resulting in the maturation of human intelligence blended with spiritual understanding. This elevating principle, called sattva, allows for the possession of balance and equanimity, permitting peace and harmony to visit the soul. A taste of this condition is enough to cause an aspiring being to set foot upon a path which will eventually lead to total illumination of consciousness. After the experience of sattva sets in, the mind loses its propensity for all types of ego-oriented activity. Perceiving the blessed Universal Mother at work in all modes of existence, humility, reverence and dedication to higher ideals become the standards in life. Inertia is transformed into peaceful respite, frantic activity turns into selfless work for the good of others, and positivity, compassion, kindness and other qualities of the balanced mind pave the way for the acquisition of transcendent experience.

It is in this way that the Divine Mother of the Universe raises human consciousness from lower truth to higher Truth. The crescent moon, the half moon and the full moon, symbolizing the waxing and waning of cyclic patterns, brings both insight and patience. Knowing that the Mother's presence guides all events and that She is the ruler of time, space and causation, Her devotees remain immersed in contemplation upon Her. If the moment is inauspicious, they bide their time and look to Her for a sign, nor will they act prematurely at a partially auspicious moment. When the full moon of Her Grace floods the heart, they know that they will be prompted by a power beyond all human understanding to attain the goal of their individual lives. Until then, as the crescent moon gradually waxes, they immerse themselves in Her work on the battlefield of relativity in order to remove the ignorance from the collective minds of humanity.

16

Her Radiant Blackness

Darkness which Illumines

Among the many powerful symbolisms associated with Mother Kali's appearance, the deep black color of Her skin captures the attention, turning it towards thoughts of transcendence and infinity. Philosophically speaking, Her dark color signifies the formlessness of *Nirguna Brahman,* the Absolute Reality without attributes. Formless Reality is often described as a static condition, thereby communicating a sense of sterility, a state void of qualities and attributes. Whereas this condition is certainly one of the modes of the nondual Brahman, to restrict It to this state alone is to limit Its vast possibilities and potentials. There is, for instance, Sri Ramakrishna's opinion on the matter: *"Brahman is both formless and endowed with form. It is beyond both of these conditions and is much more besides"* (Gospel of Sri Ramakrishna). It is here, in the mind's striving for comprehension of Brahman, that the dark color of Kali provides essential understanding.

Many thinkers, in their rush to relegate the nondual condition of pure Awareness to a state beyond name and form, end up describing Brahman as a lifeless void devoid of all qualities. Yet the scriptures describe Brahman to be of the very nature of pervasive omniscience, perpetual existence, eternal contentedness, integral knowledge, absolute freedom and infinite realization. These are not superimposed attributes but the essential constitution of

Brahman, which is not a sterile void (*shunya*) but an
infinite and spontaneous ocean of intelligent awareness, full of all perfect qualities (*purna*). In the
Avadhuta Gita, Dattatreya, a perfect knower of
Brahman, explains this condition from the standpoint of transcendence and mature renunciation:

> *I am neither of the nature of the void*
> *nor of the nature of the nonvoid,*
> *neither of pure nature nor of impure nature,*
> *neither form nor formlessness.*
> *I am the supreme Reality*
> *of the form of Its own nature.*

Being of the form of Its own nature, it is easy to
accept that God is purna, full and complete. This
explains Sri Ramakrishna's precious words which
describe that Ultimate Being as endowed with form,
immersed in formlessness, yet not restricted to
either mode and capable of operating through both
conditions while simultaneously transcending them
both. Acceptance is important in this regard, for so
much doubt, confusion and difference of opinion
resulting in endless suffering, misery and violence
can thereby be avoided. All approaches to Reality
must be consummated by attaining this comprehensive understanding. Then only can direct spiritual experience be enjoyed by struggling human
beings. Seeking can then be transformed into seeing, striving into arriving, searching into finding.
  With this final declaration of the fullness of
Consciousness affirmed, one can better understand

both the import and the significance of the Divine Mother and the meaning of Her black complexion. Hers is a darkness that is vibrating with bliss, an effulgence that is pulsating with radiance. In Her, the Truth is never harsh and difficult to gaze upon, as is the case with the sun. Instead, the Truth reflects through Her as light through a prism, casting soothing beams of light like the moon. She attracts the bold and courageous with these scintillating rays the way an ocean lures bathers. At a distance, the ocean is an attractive blue, beautiful to behold. Upon close inspection, however, the waters are seen to be clear and pristine, delightful to the touch. Therefore, Mother Kali's dark appearance, compelling and alluring at first sight, is known to contain the clear transparency of Truth to those who draw near. Both abiding Realities — the fascinating manifestation of Her form and the indivisible continuity of Her formless condition — contain Her imperceptibly subtle essence. Perceive them both as different expressions of the same Reality, and enlightenment is reached with ease. It is a dark color that is obtained by the mingling of all colors.

Mother Kali, then, blends all modes and all expressions within Her. This is why She is called the *Deva Devi Svarupaya*, the essence of all divinities. What is achieved by coalescing all possibilities is that one indivisible Reality, the sum total of all existence. In this primordial blackness dwells the ultimate Truth. Out of this primordial blackness comes an infinite manifestation. Expression finds new meaning with the Universal Mother, for She tests the limits of Her inherent powers but finds no end to them due to the eternal nature of Her Reality. Like liquid gold, out of which is fashioned an infinite variety of gold objects, She is the essence from which all expressions spring, the screen against which the projected pictures of life reveal their meaning, the proverbial thread on which the pearls of universal manifestation rest in real continuity.

Such a blackness, then, is the fertile womb of endless potential, which itself is of one essence. Ramprasad, the poet and devotee of Kali, awed by the radiant darkness of Her being, sings about its significance in several of his wisdom songs:

> There are many subtle hues of blackness,
> but Her bright complexion
> is the sheer mystery that is utterly black,
> overwhelmingly black, wonderfully black.
> When She awakens the lotus shrine
> within the secret heart,
> Her blackness is the mystic illumination
> that causes the twelve-petal blossom there
> to glow more intensely than embers.
> Her lovely Form is the incomparable Kali-black,
> blacker than the king of Death.
> Whoever has gazed upon Her potent blackness
> falls eternally in love
> and feels no attraction to any other.

Other devotees of the Divine Mother of the Universe have experienced similar experiences.

Kamalakanta, hinting at Her boundless essence, cites an entire spectrum of color to intimate Her expansive nature.

Often I wonder, is my Mother Kali really black?
My mind has become illumined by meditating
on Her black form, clothed in space.
People say that She is black,
but my mind tells me She is not always so.
She is sometimes white, sometimes yellow,
and sometimes even blue or red.
Before, I did not know what Mother was and
reflecting on Her my whole life has passed away.
But now I know Her secret –
that She is sometimes male, sometimes female
and sometimes beyond all form entirely.
Kamalakanta is amazed to see
how Shiva has become mad with ecstasy
by meditating on Her radiant splendor![14]

The Divine Mother, then, abides in Her own formless essence, but delights in playful expression. The colors of an endless array of manifestation all arise out of the unified and indivisible foundation of Her radiant blackness. Her dark complexion is the Love-filled, Peace-filled, Truth-filled essence of Reality that illumined beings call *Satchitananda* or Brahman. These same beings, immersed in that Reality, call It *Samadhi, Nirvana, Moksha, Mukti* or *Kaivalya.* It is the essential foundation upon which philosophers base their systems of learning (the essence of wisdom), the same Reality by which the lovers of God experience bliss (the essence of love), and the identical supreme personality through which beings inhabiting terrestrial realms gain eventual fulfillment (the essence of selfless works).

Therefore, it is seen that the Divine Mother of the Universe and Her black complexion represent pure conscious Awareness and its myriad of expressions. Her all-encompassing effulgent darkness contains both these modes of existence, like the black void of space supports an infinite number of planets and suns. As the transparent background She is the witness of all phenomena as well as the animating principle Itself. The seers call these "Two who are One" by the names of Brahman and Shakti. Goddess Kali, the Universal Mother, is interchangeable with both these aspects of Reality, representing both the transcendent wisdom mode *(Shiva)* and the dynamic animating principle *(Shakti)* in turns and simultaneously. It is no wonder that the poet/sage, Ramprasad, sings:

> *Who is this Transcendent Woman*
> *striding on the heart of Absolute Reality?*
> *Her sublime form, blacker than the blackest storm,*
> *streams with blood like vermilion blossoms...*
> *The vast tangle of Her black tresses,*
> *flowing freely like the darkness of the breaking storm,*
> *dispel with their radiance all negation and despair*

It is into this infinite blackness that the universe and all its living creatures disappear with boundless ecstasy at the time of final dissolution.

17

Her Long Black Flowing Hair

The Intoxicating Scent of Boundless Freedom

Unbounded Freedom, Indivisible Unity and Absolute Truth, these three precious qualities are the essence of spiritual life. Of these three, freedom is epitomized by the trailing luxuriant tresses of Goddess Kali, whose supreme will is unalterable in all accounts except by Her. Sri Sarada Devi speaks about this powerful will of the Mother by stating, *"What the hand of destiny has written can just as easily be erased by Her."*[15] We can infer by this revealing statement that destiny is not a fixed quotient but a relative law that can be altered. This is accomplished either by the act of self-surrender to the Lord or by the bestowal of Grace due to the Universal Mother's intervention. This is an exciting revelation and a useful insight, for discovering this truth frees human beings from bondage, whether it be self-imposed or inherent in nature. This allows them to merge with their primal essence.

The color of Mother's dark complexion has already been discussed. It represents an initial unity which contains all modes of expression. This blackness that is total, that is absolute, is also a property of Her beautiful hair that flows unimpeded and untrammeled throughout space. Thus, freedom shares the characteristics of unity. They might as well be synonymous terms. In fact, truth, unity and freedom are all one because the characteristics that they share are such qualities as indivisibility, eternity and immortality. Swami Vivekananda gives testament to the Universal Mother by speaking about Her supreme will which possesses these attributes:

> *Is it inherent nature? Something uncreate?*
> *Or destiny? Some unforeseen result? –*
> *who, lacking nothing, is accountable,*
> *whose chain of will, untrammeled, grasps the laws.*
> *May She, the Primal Guide, my shelter be.*[16]

Freedom, besides being an essential ingredient in spiritual life, is also a sign of arrival, of realization. Those who possess an unrestricted spirit are the true divine workers on earth, effecting positive change by revealing to struggling beings their immortal nature and encouraging them to take refuge there.

Comprehension of the condition of spiritual freedom is far more meaningful and beneficial than any interpretation expressed in the world's dogmatic religious approaches. Here, in these narrow hallways, human beings are forced to conform to fit into one convenient mold. So much the better for those who, having no hold upon freedom themselves, are still zealous to give it or withhold it from others. The "one size fits all" method allows such pretenders to disguise their lack of freedom in a maze of confusing jargon that, as Swami Vivekananda says, "*accomplishes little more than to work up a froth about the lips!*" Criticizing the more liberal approaches which emphasize personal freedom and direct communion with the Divine Being, in whatever way the aspirant views It, these questionable authorities mix myth and fiction with half-truths, creating a philosophical concoction that is a misrepresentation of the universal laws of religion. This is misleading and eventually gives rise to dissension, violence, war, genocide, poverty, famine, plague and digression of evolution, generally in that order.

This charade, this chimera and its horrible outcome, is an agonizing dream through which passes that segment of humanity who are entirely bereft of reason, compassion and unified understanding. These beings, some of whom may even declare their allegiance to the Lord, are tied hand and foot to materialism by the strands of desire, karmic repercussion and a selfish urge to prosper at the expense of their fellow human beings. Be it an exploitation of a physical nature involving monetary gain, or a gluttony for power over the minds and bodies of human beings, the result is all the same. It is mock concern and insincerity masquerading as the real article. The inexorable laws of nature will duly have their effect on such as these, for the Lord does not abide with the insincerity of hypocrites or charlatans.

On the opposite side of the issue dwell the Universal Mother's legions, those who are purely dedicated to the blessed Lord of the Universe. This divine figure is always one, but appears in different forms with different names throughout time. This being is called *Ishvara* in Sanskrit, and the appearance of powerful incarnations, all drawn from one eternal Soul and appearing as different emanations, comes from It. Ishvara, the personal God, is the

Lord of the Universe, the principle of God with form that is one of the Divine Mother's expressions. Ishvara and the inseparable emanations that spring from It are eternally free. They reside, as it were, in the long flowing hair of Mother Kali that permeates the universe, giving it cohesiveness and lending it life and radiance. Therefore, incarnations such as Rama, Krishna, Buddha, Christ and others, to name a few, are the Universal Mother's free agents, ever one with Her but unleashed upon the realm of name and form to effect positive change and help beings fulfill the purpose of their existence.

On the relative plane of existence, where revelations of a nondual nature are rare, their truths less obvious, the Divine Mother's black hair takes on a more practical meaning in order to aid those caught in the fundamental trap of duality. Here, on earth, where human beings are convinced of their mortality due to attachment to names and forms, belief and faith are hard to come by. Though the Mother's divine emissaries are present in greater and lesser manifestations, their freedom to transmit spiritual insight and realization is hampered due to the impediments which inhibit the minds of struggling beings. The way out of this maze can only be effected by acquiring courage and fortitude, as this is the way leading to freedom. The vision of Mother Kali's wild tresses, free and unbound, confers a sense of boldness and bravery upon those caught in the maze of relativity and gives them the desire and stamina needed to snap the bonds of *Maya*. This is why the poet/saint, Ramprasad, sings devoutly:

Her Eyes of Mercy and Power are like moon and sun,
Her Third Eye of Wisdom
like Cosmic Fire at the end of a world-cycle.
Her Forehead bears crescent moon
and vermilion dot of consecration.
Her Earrings assume the form of dead infants,
emblem of Her Renunciation of birth and death.
Her constant Smile
is the lightning flash of full Enlightenment.
The abundant black Hair that tumbles to Her Feet
is Her Power of Transformation.
Ecstatic sages circle around Her Sweetness
as intoxicated bees about a lotus.

Whether by sterling example, then, or by spiritual camaraderie, or by divine intervention, the Divine Mother of the Universe always succeeds in freeing Her votaries from the entrapments of illusion. Spiritual emancipation, the liberation of the embodied being from the clutches of egotism, suffering and death, is Her divine mission, for all sparks of Consciousness are Hers, forming one blazing bonfire of inseparable Awareness. The radiant darkness of Her skin, the inspiring flow of black hair, the black moon on Her brow, these symbols of infinity shake the mind, releasing it from its habitual preoccupation with things mundane. After liberation from such bondage is attained through Her Grace, the soul takes flight towards the source of this awesome presence. At this auspicious moment, another important symbol makes its appearance, lending new and ever-fresh meaning to Her radiant blackness.

18

Swarms of Bees about Her Hair

The Ceaseless Sound of Perpetual Bliss

The soul of every human being, that complex of transmigrating consciousness which occupies various body/mind mechanisms, strives, through one means or another, to unite with the unseen source of creation. Inherent in the mind's makeup, however veiled or submerged that knowledge may be, lies the awareness that life in the universe, amidst its many aspects of existence, is not a coincidence. It is, in fact, fraught with an infinite set of possibilities which all proceed from and are orchestrated by a Supreme Intelligence. In most, the search for this ultimate Reality is weak or nonexistent. This is due, in part, to the bundles of mental impressions which lie unnoticed and unheeded in the mind amidst its subconscious layers. Some of these are dormant, buried deep in the unconscious, while others abide near the surface and even become activated and on the conscious level. This complex of congealed thought energy forms a part of what we call the personality which is shaped and influenced by desires, attachments, previous actions and past associations. This, the lower self known as the ego, is what unawakened beings identify with as their essential being.

When this kind of misidentification occurs, human awareness gets saturated with ego-consciousness, a sense of narrow individualism which permeates all activities and experiences of life with its banal presence. Even the natural faculties one is born with which are present in the mind and intellect are negatively influenced by this clever usurper. As a result, the clear light of pure Consciousness, the rightful monarch of the human kingdom which becomes revealed in the sheath of refined intelligence, gets obscured. This process is mentioned by Bhagavan Sri Krishna in the *Bhagavad Gita*:

Knowledge is covered, O beloved,
by the insatiable fire of selfish desire,
and the senses, the mind, and the intellect
are said to be its seat;
by these it deludes mankind
by veiling his wisdom.

Under the misleading influence of ego-oriented action and the repercussions coming from them due to inexorable universal laws, the spiritual nature of all things which beings sense or intuit goes unheeded and undeveloped, buried under layers of impurity and superimposition. Transmigrating souls laboring under this burden of egotism thereby relegate the kingdom of the Spirit to an inferior position. This destroys any opportunity for the development and maturation of a beneficial spiritual life. As Ramprasad Sen sings, these beings *"consume earth instead of nectar."* Sri Ramakrishna states, *"flies land on both sweets and filth, but bees land on flowers and sip only honey."* Such is the nature of some bees that they will duly select a particular type of flower which produces and bears the rarest and sweetest nectar and only frequent that variety. In the realm of spirituality, it is the children of the Universal Mother who most resemble these discriminating bees, drinking the nectar of immortality from the highest source possible. These selfless ones transcend the illusion associated with the ego complex and embrace unity instead. As Sri Sarada Devi, the Holy Mother, has emphasized in Her teachings, *"Forgetting your personality, remember your true Self."*

In iconographic representations of Mother Kali, one of the most striking and exhilarating features of Her complex appearance is the multitude of bees that swarm about Her beautiful black hair. A constant and intoxicating drone of the sacred sounds *AUM, HRIM,* and other mystical emanations sacred to the Goddess, proceeds from their intense activity as they dip and glide in and out of the Universal Mother's dark, fragrant tresses. The *Srimad Devi Bhagavatam* describes this unique vision as follows:

> *She was resplendent with the brilliance of ten million suns and looked beautiful like ten million Kandarpas (gods of love). Her body was anointed with variegated colors and She wore fine clothing. A wonderful garland was suspended from Her neck, Her body was decked with various ornaments and in the fists of Her hands were wonderful rows of large black bees. Her one hand was ready to grant boons and Her other hand was ready to hold out 'no fear.' On the neck of Bhagavati, the ocean of Mercy, and peaceful,*

were seen the variegated garlands with large black bees all around. Those male and female bees were singing incessantly all around Her the Hrimkara Mantra (the first vibration of force). Kotis of black bees surrounded Her.

These fortunate winged insects symbolize the many individual souls occupying subtle space. They have been freed from the mundane constrictions and preoccupations characteristic of beings attached to the earthly plane. Though they still retain a slight trace of their individual existence, ideas and attractions associated with superficial existence bound up with limited pleasures and base sensuality have been effaced completely. These soaring souls are actually sheaths of enlightened intelligence that have been purged of binding impressions, those whose consciousness has been refined of burdensome concepts and restricting impediments. The weighty tendencies that once bound these elevated souls to the earth, to the idea that life is a matter of mere bodily existence experienced through the limited vehicles of the five senses, are gone. They have been replaced by an exalted state of being that identifies only with bliss, truth, love and freedom, for these are the abiding conditions of true existence.

Like whales, which take delight by diving into the depths of the ocean and sporting and breaching on its surface as well, these black bees of Mother Kali's *Mahalila* enjoy both the bliss of immersion and the play of apparent separation. Plunging into the expanse of Her dark, flowing hair, their black bodies become virtually indistinguishable from Her thick locks — a union that brings inexpressible joy. This is the bliss associated with the total loss of individuality. Then, rebounding from this state of complete immersion and identity with Reality, they arch high into the atmosphere of timeless awareness which always permeates Mother Kali's presence, only to gain further ecstasy from repeated submersions. Thus does the infinite and inexpressible play of free and boundless awareness continue.

This perpetual and playful expression throws revelatory light upon the inexpressible nature of the Supreme Being. To comprehend the secrets of this play is to be forever free of any binding notions about the nature of Reality. This state is devoid of such peculiar ideas that Reality is a void, bereft of expression, or that It is merely a condition of duality where beings remain separate from God, enjoying heavenly existence in a mode of individual existence. Perceiving clearly that Reality is at once the combined essence of all experience and simultaneously transcendent of all experience causes the mind to rest forever in a sublime condition of Peace. This is the *"Peace which passeth all understanding,"* for It is not limited by concepts of form or formlessness, void or voidlessness, and other conceptual restrictions.

This innate unity which forms the immutable ground for both dynamic expression and transcendent equipoise is revealed in the words of the Kali

Avatar, Sri Ramakrishna, who states, *"Brahman and Shakti are One."* He called this limitless Being, *"Ma,"* explaining that when this indivisible Reality is busy creating, preserving and dissolving the universe It is called Shakti, and when It is resting in Its own nondual condition, choosing not to manifest Its boundless potential for infinite expression It is called Brahman.

The soul-bees abiding in the sacred presence of Mother Kali know the nature of this Reality, the secret of eternal oneness, for they are ever plunging into Its essence and withdrawing themselves in turns, fully conscious that both modes are expressions of one indivisible Reality. These are Her precious spiritual children who have transcended illusion and escaped from the net of maya — that web of ego-oriented action whose sticky strands bind unillumined beings to terrestrial concerns of mundane import. Free from attachment to relativity and liberated from the kind of narrow thinking which declares Reality to be limited in any way, they exercise their divine right to express true freedom. This is also called *Ananda,* a bliss replete with all divine qualities, inexpressible and inexhaustible. Its other name, immortality, though often shorn of Its true meaning due to the narrow understanding of institutionalized religion, expresses well the boundless feeling of those who have gained the nondual realm of truth, unity and freedom. Only those who have directly experienced this timeless essence can understand the unique spiritual mystery shared by those who seek to gather the precious nectar of spiritual emancipation. Dwelling forever in that sweet and sublime state, they seldom emerge to give away such secrets, for those who cannot conceive of it will never believe in it.

Still, for the sake of beings caught in the fundamental web of delusion due to karmic repercussions and cosmic laws, an occasional large black bee, legs laden with the pollen of nondual Truth, leaves the ecstatic play of bliss and settles in the elemental region of this material earth, intent upon disseminating knowledge. Sri Ramakrishna described this phenomenon by saying, *"The bee becomes silent when it sits on the flower, content with drinking deep of its nectar, but it also occasionally hums and buzzes, drunk with delight."* The humming sound which emanates from this extraordinary bee represents the teachings coming from the fully illumined soul who, not content with enjoying bliss in private, undertakes to share it with struggling humanity so that they might know their true nature and come to enjoy the experience of enlightenment. Such a being is the essence of compassion, epitomizing the very nature of freedom.

In the selfless hearts of these exemplars of Truth, we find that the Mother's loving kindness and boundless grace are made manifest, for they are huge reservoirs of love and compassion. Words fail to describe their dedication and sacrifice, and words also fail to express the gratitude of those who receive this unalloyed Love which flows from these

infinite receptacles of Mother's Grace. When these
large black bees of compassion have finally com-
pleted their mission, depositing the pollen of nondual Truth on the screen of the world's sincere
yearning for realization and enlightenment, they
return to the Mother's long, flowing hair of untrammeled freedom, dissolving into their essence once
again. As Kamalakanta, the lover of Mother Kali
sings:

> *The black Bee of my mind*
> *has become completely absorbed*
> *in the dark Lotus Feet of Mother Kali.*
> *Other flowers, the sensual blossoms of this earth,*
> *have now lost their hypnotic attraction.*
> *Her Feet are black, the bee too is black,*
> *the two have become indistinguishable!*
> *Witnessing the intoxicating influence*
> *of this divine absorption, the five senses,*
> *ashamed of their limited inebriation,*
> *cease to function and the five elements*
> *dissolve into their primal source.*
> *Kamalakanta, beholding this phenomenon,*
> *perceives all as equal,*
> *and discarding both happiness and misery,*
> *swims in a brimming ocean of ecstatic bliss*
> *forever.*[17]

19

Mother Kali's Female Attendants

Her Triumphant Legions

The Divine Mother of the Universe is named Kali, a name that suggests the Supreme Goddess who is the witness of everything within the domain of time, space and causality. She not only oversees the activity occurring within the entire universe, She creates and permeates the three worlds as well. Finally, Her name infers a vast and timeless essence that transcends all phenomenal manifestation. In Her boundless omniscience, She embodies and wields all powers which proceed from this timeless essence. Her array of helpers are legion. She calls upon a host of emanations, divine attendants and dedicated workers to assist Her in the universal process and to execute Her supreme will in the battle between negative and positive forces. Thus has She become known as the *Deva Devi Svarupaya* — *the* essence of all gods and goddesses.

Mother Kali epitomizes the unified whole, the subtle basis for both dynamism and transcendence. Within this cohesive superstructure, which is ultimately indivisible or ever-uniform, the *Mahavidya Mahamaya Devi* exercises confounding powers in order to divide and subdivide Her powers profusely. The *Srimad Devi Bhagavatam* describes Her activities as fourfold. As the Sattvika Devi She preserves the three worlds and protects the peoples of Her design. As the Rajasika Devi She animates the lifeforce of all beings and propels them into repetitious cycles of intense activity. As the Tamasika Devi She destroys all that She has wrought, dissolving all names and forms back into their primal essence once again. It is in the fourth aspect that Her ultimate power resides. As Nirguna Devi She abides in blissful equipoise beyond all modes of expression, resting still and supine in subtle splendor.

These far-reaching activities that the Devi engages in are actually all managed by Her powers, while She remains ever detached and unaffected by any cosmic law or process. Thus it is that we read in the *Bhagavad Gita* that all action is actually performed by Prakriti: "*The Gunas of Prakriti perform all karma. With the intellect clouded by delusion man thinks 'I am the doer.'*" Therefore, the three gunas — sattvas, rajas and tamas — are all powers of the Universal Mother, dependent upon Her control and supervision. Thus, Sri Krishna explains:

And whatever beings are of Sattva,
of Rajas or of Tamas,
know them to proceed from Me;
still I am not in them, they are in Me.
Deluded by the threefold dispositions of Prakriti
— the Gunas — this world does not know Me,
who am above them and immutable.

Apart from Her powers springing from insentient nature are Her emanations. These are difficult to categorize, for the power of Mahamaya is complex and inscrutable. In the physical universe, portions of Her terrestrial body comprised of matter and energy have diminished to subatomic proportions, and this is only a single aspect of Her infinite nature. On subtler levels, in the realm of the heart and mind where human relations and interactions are of paramount importance, the Universal Mother appears in many forms. The primordial Goddess who is ultimately One, is said to manifest in five main divisions called *Prakriti Panchaka*. These five, which the *Srimad Devi Bhagavatam* calls *Mula Prakriti,* the root power of all expression, are singled out as Durga, Lakshmi, Sarasvati, Savitri and Radha — the Goddesses of transforming power, beauty and abundance, pervasive intelligence, spiritual growth and supreme bliss. These main aspects retain the power to further separate into parts and each of these parts can divide into parts of parts.

The ability and power of the Goddess in this matter is infinite and unsurpassed. What is most amazing is Her innate uniformity, for She remains undivided despite these many transformations and unattached amidst all activity. What is no less wonderful is the spectacle of Her multifarious emanations. The *Srimad Devi Bhagavatam* speaks of Her prowess and infinite power by citing one of Her unprecedented appearances: *"In ancient times, the Goddess Bhadra Kali, the destroyer of Daksha's sacrifice, appeared in hideous forms, surrounded by hundreds and thousands of Yoginis."* The Yoginis mentioned here are only one class of sixty who serve Mother Kali.

Other mentions are made as well with regard to the attendants of the Supreme Goddess. As an example of the multiplying power of the Goddess, the story of the appearance and disappearance of Sati Devi on the world scene has become famous. Due to Her father's verbal abuse of Lord Shiva, Sati burnt Her body in the fire arising out of yoga. Lord Shiva, unable to bear separation from Sati, took Her body on his shoulders and roamed the worlds lamenting Her loss. In order to free Lord Shiva from his sorrow, Bhagavan Vishnu severed Sati's body into 108 parts with his arrows. Wherever a part of Sati's body fell, a place of pilgrimage associated with the Goddess was created. Thus is the Goddess worshipped with 108 different names.

In battle, the superior warrioress, Goddess Kali, calls upon Her divine attendants to assist in the destruction of evil. Varying classes of helpers may appear, according to the need and situation. At times, the shaktis of the gods themselves attend the battlefield, each one being a full representation of the lordly power possessed by their divine husbands. From Indra, the lord of the gods, springs Indrani, bearing the thunderbolt and riding on the back of Airavata, the divine elephant. From the primal creator, Brahma, emanates Brahmani, riding majestically on the back of a swan and sporting a magical set of holy beads. From Vishnu, the benign preserver, comes Vaishnavi, wearing yellow robes and riding the Garuda, possessing the weapons of conch, discus, mace and lotus. From Lord Shiva, the Devi Shankari appears, riding a white bull and bearing snakes, bracelets and trident while sporting the mudra of fearlessness. The wife of Kartikeya named Kaumari enters the battlefield mounted on a beautiful peacock. Others too, make an appearance, like the goddess Varahi, resembling a female boar and riding boldly on departed spirits *(pretas)*, and Narasimhi, the wife of Narasimha, the half-man, half-lion manifestation. Even the shakti of Lord Yama, the god of death, enters the fray, mounted on a buffalo and bearing an invincible staff, for her services will be in high demand. The list of divine emanations from the primal Shakti is endless.

Away from the external battlefield, amidst the subtler atmosphere of thoughts, ideals and qualities, the Goddess is no less proficient and prolific. She is capable of assuming the energy of any divine attribute, for it is Her presence that creates and bestows these precious boons. These qualities become manifest in the hearts and minds of all beings due to good actions and selfless service. The list of them is too lengthy to enumerate. The major parts of the main aspects of the Goddess are familiar to all though. Goddesses such as Ganga Devi, the power of purification, and Tulsi, the energy of healing, top the list. These are followed by important aspects like Manasa, who epitomizes perfection through austerity and Shasthi, the very essence of nurturing motherhood. Mangala Chandika's powers manifest through the destruction of all obstacles and the performance of good works for the sake of

others, while Maheshvari Kali embodies the fullness
of absolute power and astounding resilience.
Finally, there is the Devi Vasundhara, the goddess of
this earth, who supplies food stuffs to all beings and
creates jewels and precious ores as well.

From these parts of the *Mula Prakriti* come the
issues from the parts. Names such as Svaha, the
wife of fire, who allows and sanctions the act of
offering oblations, and Svadha, the one who causes
the sacred offering to be fruitful, are well known.
Dakshina and Diksha, the wives of sacrifice, are
worshipped and honored everywhere, for they provide just recompense for those who are versed in
sacred ritual and graced with special talents. Svasti
is also important due to Her ability to grant the
desire and will power to perform action. Pusti and
Tusti are revered because they grant nourishment
and satisfaction respectively. Without them there
would be no growth or happiness. Sampatti gives
freedom from poverty while Dhriti grants patience.
Sati Devi epitomizes precious friendship while Daya
Devi bestows the treasure of mercy and hope.
Pratistha Devi and Punya Devi grant notoriety and
merit and the goddess Kirti bestows fame. Kriya
Devi beckons all to action and presides over the
righteous performance of all activities while
Shraddha Devi transmits faith. Other aspects of the
Goddess who appear are Shanti Devi (peace),
Buddhi Devi (intelligence), Murti Devi (beauty) and
Bhakti Devi (devotion). Additional attributes asso-
ciated with the Goddess are sleep, time, hunger,

thirst, fire, death, old age, lassitude, pleasure, satisfaction and many others.   Finally, the presiding power of the Goddess that manifests in the animals (cows, horses, elephants, etc.), in nature (sun, moon, water, plants etc.) and even in minor village deities, all possess a portion of that primordial energy associated with Mahavidya Mahamaya Devi.

The Dasamahavidyas

No list of the divine attendants of the Universal Mother would be complete without mention of the *Dasamahavidyas,* the ten direct emanations of the Supreme Goddess. The term, *Mahavidya* translates as "Supreme Knowledge," so these ten aspects represent all that is known and can ever be known. These integral parts of the Divine Mother are inseparable, though their activities apply to different areas of universal manifestation. Their names are Kali, Tara, Shodashi, Bhuvaneshvari, Bhairavi, Chinnamasta, Dhumavati, Bagala, Matangi and Kamala.

I
Kali

Kali herself is the first, the Goddess who directs all matters pertaining to the march of time. The appearance of the concept of time in the mind, its passage, and its eventual disappearance after the cosmic cycle ends — these aspects of all-seeing, all-devouring time are manipulated by Mother Kali. As the eternal witness of all activities in the universe, the Divine Mother Kali is able to see into every aspect of the creation, guiding it through its phases and dissolving it in the end. The importance of Her presence is understood more clearly when She is perceived from this standpoint, for it is seen that She is responsible for both the destruction of the universe, a function which narrow minds often limit Her to, and for its growth, especially pertaining to spiritual matters which are the area of Her special expertise. Transformation of human nature — from animal to heroic, from heroic to divine[18] — that is Her chief purpose as far as relativity is concerned, and it is a most important function. Add to that Her ability to liberate the transmigrating soul from its attachment to and involvement with ego-oriented existence, and a comprehensive picture of this Supreme Goddess is revealed. In this regard, not only are time and space Her territory, but Yama, the lord of death, provides his service due to Her direction as well. Thus is the supreme importance of Mother Kali recognized by all spiritual luminaries and particularly by the devotees of the Divine Mother.

II
Tara

The second Mahavidya, Tara, is close to Mother Kali, possessing some of the same attributes associated with Her. She blends two seemingly opposed qualities within Her and expresses them both perfectly. Primarily, She epitomizes the boundlessness of open space, both in its personal and impersonal aspects. Like Mother Kali, She embodies the void of primal space from which all things emerge. Kali and Tara contain all manifestations within them much like the midnight firmament acts as a backdrop for thousands of shining stars. In fact, Tara is directly associated with *Hiranyagarbha*, often referred to as the golden embryo or cosmic egg in Vedanta science. Far more than just physical space, the Hiranyagarbha is cosmic intelligence, the Supreme Lord of the universe who projects the subtle and physical worlds. Again, the bodies of all creatures that inhabit this creation come from this act of projection. Therefore, Tara is often indicated by the Sanskrit term, *samasti-sukshma-sarirabhimani,* the sum total of all subtle bodies. On a more intimate level, Goddess Tara is well-known for Her boundless compassion. In this way, Her boundlessness applies to both Her formless nature and to Her deep concern for all creatures. Ramprasad sings of Her double purpose in his wisdom songs:

> *The scriptures of the Goddess solemnly declare:*
> *'Tara is formless.*
> *She is the clear light beyond all forms.'*
> *But this poet madly responds:*
> *Mother exists also as each life form.*
> *Open your foolish eyes*
> *and perceive the Holy Mother everywhere.*
> *Even the darkness of this world is simply Her Light.'*[19]

This wisdom song reveals that Mother Tara is both immanent and transcendent, appearing in both modes to accommodate the different attitudes of Her precious spiritual children. Due to the widespread fame of Her compassionate nature, Mother Tara has come to epitomize caring and concern for all sentient beings, making Her an object of refuge and reverence for Hindus and Buddhists alike. As a result, in the minds of devotees and scholars, the impersonal and the transcendental has been relegated more to Mother Kali's domain. Ramprasad, who recognizes no essential distinction between the aspects of the Goddess, sings to this issue with deep insight:

> Take me in Your Arms of Love.
> Encircle me with Your radiant Presence.
> Manifest Your gentle aspect as Tara
> with Her delicate Smile,
> clad in the rainbow silk of peacefulness.
> Tara is the Dawn of Mercy, Kali the Night of Mystery.
> O Goddess, this child has contemplated
> Your awesome Aspect so intensely.
> Put down Your terrible Sword.
> Drown me in Your tender Delight.

III
Shodashi

Shodashi, the third major aspect of the Universal Mother, is purity incarnate. Her name, which translates as "She who is eternally sixteen," transmits an aura of youth and vitality blended with the immaculate nature of a young virgin. The result is a Goddess of divine character, taintless and perfect in both action and introspection. She is Purna Devi, the Goddess who embodies all beneficial qualities in the fullest possible sense. Her nature is full and complete, lacking nothing and so desiring nothing. Innocence, guilelessness, equanimity and serenity — these are some of Her foremost attributes. The aspect of Shodashi has been perfectly expressed in this contemporary day and age through the person of Sri Sarada Devi, the Holy Mother, who was the divine consort of Sri Ramakrishna Paramahamsa, the Avatar of Kali. The Great Master once asked Sri Sarada to receive the worship intended for the sacred image on the altar, replacing the icon with Her very body. Then, while both of them were swept up in a mood of ecstasy, He worshipped Her as the living Goddess, a full emanation of the Universal Mother in human form. This famous and auspicious event took place on the traditional Shodashi Puja day, making it all the more sacred to the devotees of the Divine Mother of the Universe.

IV
Bhuvanesvari

The word, "*bhuvana,*" translates from the original Sanskrit simply as "world." Therefore, it is easy to perceive the fourth Mahavidya in Her role as the "Mother of the Worlds." Not to be limited to the material aspects of the physical world alone though,

She represents all the forces that combine to create and sustain such a realm. This indicates that She is the Mother of subtle worlds as well. In fact, if one explores the Sanskrit word *bhuva* further, another meaning is discovered, for the word *bhuvah* refers to the etheric realm which is also called the astral world. This world, *bhuvah,* is beyond the earthly plane, *bhur,* and generally corresponds with the heavens spoken of in other religious traditions. Since Her presence and power permeates these realms of existence, it is easy to understand why Her aspect is so loved and why She is propitiated and sought after by thousands of devotees. Her sacred name is often used to represent the Divine Mother of the Universe Herself, mentioned repeatedly in sacred scriptures such as the *Srimad Devi Bhagavatam.* Her direct association with the earth plane makes Her an ideal aspect of the Goddess to worship, for Her close proximity allows accessibility and communion.

V
Bhairavi

As has been seen, not all the dimensions of the Divine Mother's manifestations are positive. Many of them are terrible, being not only difficult to comprehend but also hard to accept. This is because beings tend to embrace that which is pleasant while shying away from what is not. Yet, attraction and aversion are listed in Vedantic teachings as another pair amidst the many sets of dualities which must be overcome and transcended. This is definitely one of the secrets behind the appearance of Mother's terrible aspects. She accomplishes a divine purpose through these horrific expressions. The Goddess Bhairavi embodies such a purpose, for She represents those tendencies of the human heart and mind which lead to the destruction of spiritual life. Through desires, attachments and temptations of all types, the mind is led astray and plunged into the bewitching morass of worldly existence. Thus does destruction take place, not only on a physical level, but on the plane of intelligence and spirituality as well.

What can be the purpose of such destruction? As the old adages declare, one cannot appreciate the beauty of daytime fully without the coming of nightfall. Darkness and light are complementary conditions. The same holds true of such dual conditions as knowledge and ignorance, pain and pleasure, virtue and vice, bondage and liberation, and certainly good and bad. The Devi Bhairavi, then, reveals the distinctions present in all the pairs of opposites, and by so doing, demonstrates to suffering humanity the precious nature of freedom of choice. By recognizing these distinctions and exercising the right to choose between right and wrong, suffering, which comes as a result of karmic repercussions due to good and bad actions, can be transcended. In short, no redemption would be possible without Her extreme teaching, which is meant to make a deep impression. It is simultaneously radical and noncompromising. In this light, She is revealed as an extremely important aspect of the Goddess and one that human beings can learn a valuable lesson from on all levels of their existence.

VI
Chinnamasta

Naked, holding Her own severed head in Her hands, and drinking Her own blood, the Goddess Chinnamasta, the sixth Mahavidya, is an enigma. Well worth contemplating, this aspect of the Universal Mother provides insight into both practical and esoteric knowledge. Simply put, the symbolism surrounding the severed head and the drinking of Her own blood stands for self-sustenance. On a spiritual level, the fact that She holds Her head in Her hands indicates that She is in full control of Her own mind and destiny. That She has mastered death and seen through its fundamental illusion is also illustrated by this strange spectacle, for who could remain alive without a head? Her life-blood, ebbing from the severed head, is not wasted, for She quaffs this elixir of life in easy fashion, indicating the perpetual condition of self-renewal to be Her eternal state. Her nakedness, as is the case with Mother Kali, represents total freedom from superimposition of any kind while revealing Her as the full embodiment of nondual Truth, radiant and impossible to obscure. Her message to humanity, transmitted in no uncertain terms by Her amazing appearance, is threefold, and can be summarized as follows: "life is eternal, death is an illusion, and dedication to Truth alone makes this clear."

VII
Dhumavati

Delving further into the powerful yet terrible aspects of the Universal Mother, the Goddess Dhumavati stands revealed. In Her is no lesson of choice and no second chance, at least not on a terrestrial level. The prefix of Her name, *dhuma,* means smoke, symbolizing the complete annihilation and destruction of the world by fire. Whereas Bhairavi indicates the direction in which each positive or negative action leads, Dhumavati forcefully and completely rids manifestation of all names and forms, clearly illustrating their fundamental evanescence. All structures are dissolved immediately and without the least hesitation.

As is the case with all of the Universal Mother's activities though, there is a divine purpose to Dhumavati's extreme actions. Symbolized by the ashes which lie smoking after the elemental destruction has taken place, this aspect of the Mother awakens sleeping human consciousness to the fact that only in perfect renunciation is freedom possible. All selfish grasping after transitory phenomena and all attachment to attractive physical structures or coveted mental concepts is nothing but vain delusion. It is bound to be futile in the end when all is reduced to ashes. This is why the Holy Mother, Sri Sarada Devi declared, *"All this attraction to the human frame, I do not understand it. What does this body amount to in the end? Just a few pounds of ashes, my dear. Give up all vanity associated with it."*

Goddess Dhumavati, then, teaches a lesson, and She does it through the revelation of such ideals as detachment and renunciation. She separates faltering beings from their hopeless clinging to things ephemeral, showing them, even through the hard way if necessary, that matter is transitory. She does not stop at this lesson either, but demonstrates that both life-force and the power of thought are noneternal. What happens then to selfish clinging when there is nothing to attach to? What happens to the niceties of social convention when all is ultimately destroyed in the fires of dissolution? What happens to our concept of life based upon mental speculation and fleeting experience? What is left is what is essential, what was there in the beginning, what is never lost or destroyed. Ramprasad, the awakened poet of the Mother describes this perfectly:

O mysterious Kali,
cremation grounds are Your great delight,
for there You release souls from mundane existence.
I have transformed my heart
into a cremation ground
so you will be attracted hereto dance
in ceaseless, liberating bliss.
O Goddess of Wisdom,
my limited desires have been consumed
on the vast pyre of renunciation.
O Goddess of Freedom,
I am surrounded by the ashes
that were my conventional world,
waiting for You to come.

Please manifest in the brilliant midnight hour
of this renouncing heart.

VIII
Bagala

Desires, attachments and temptations are very difficult challenges to overcome. Whereas they are often detrimental to spiritual life, especially when taken to extremes, they do have a positive side and provide impetus to relative existence. For instance, the desire for the basic amenities of life is natural to the embodied condition, and attachments to family and loved ones involving higher sentiments such as love, trust, faith and devotion play an important role in the drama of life.

With regard to desires and attachments, the same cannot always be said of conditions such as hatred, cruelty, jealousy, anger, greed, selfishness and other completely negative passions. These are nearly always detrimental, though some good may come out of them occasionally. Bagala, the crane-headed goddess and the eighth Mahavidya who attends the Divine Mother of the Universe, is the mistress of this domain. The dark side of human nature, filled with animalistic propensities and other unrefined elements, is Her specialty. This makes Her a feared aspect to contemplate, for a devotee that approaches and peers into Her portal of darkness risks sanity itself.

Still, like other aspects of the Universal Mother, Bagala is intent on a divine purpose. Her presence reveals the need for purification, and it is only when the dark emotions like rage, lust and the others raise their ugly heads that they can be apprehended and destroyed. At other times, they lie hidden deep in the fabric of human nature, disguised by less erratic emotions or masked by pleasant facades. The powerful Goddess Bagala not only forces such poison to the surface, utilizing just the right moment to display it, but also reveals ways to neutralize it completely. This occurs only to those who have developed a little potential for growth within them or to those whom the Goddess specially selects for Her own hidden purposes.

Thus does this enigmatic Goddess perform an essential function in the Divine Mother's realm. By bringing these obscure and undesirable parts of human nature into the light, She allows us to encounter them and neutralize their effects, much as one might defang a cobra. Without Her animating presence, human beings would never receive the opportunity to purge themselves of these ugly habits and tendencies lurking beneath the surface of consciousness. If this were the case, that all-important march to the high citadel of nondual Truth would be impossible, for no sooner would the ascent begin then one of these negative passions would rise to the surface and cause a fall. Therefore, the Divine Mother of the Universe knows Her business well and allocates every dimension of Her creation to the adept management of a particular aspect suited for Her ultimate purpose. By attention to detail, however small or unpleasant, the

Universal Mother brings all beings to their fullest potential and reveals to them their highest destiny.

IX
Matangi

It has been said that power is the most intoxicating substance, and those who are drunk with its distorting influence often act as proof of this statement. In earthly realms and spiritual dimensions as well, the desire for power perverts many beings and destroys many higher aspirations. Whether the desires concentrate around material wealth or occult powers, the result is often the same. The attainment of power nearly always results in a need to control, and this tendency insidiously extends itself into all areas of life at all levels of existence.

Matangi is the Goddess who epitomizes the power of domination, and being such, captures the consciousness of all who would exercise control over the world and its creatures. These beings, mesmerized under the spell of gaining power, may believe that they are acting under the impetus of their own individual will, but they are completely mistaken. Matangi has them fully under Her control, for dominion over all the worlds is Her game, the act of domination, Her expertise. Therefore, She is subtly present in the minds of these misguided beings, even as that initial inkling of longing to bring others under their control. Being so subtle, She brings all such desires to an end, either swiftly or in a timely fashion, depending upon the ends which suit Her divine purpose.

As can well be imagined, this aspect of the Universal Mother expresses a positive side to Her art. All beings who strive for perfection, whether in spiritual or secular domains, receive Her guidance, for She delights at seeing the well-intentioned reach their goals by gaining control of the very things which bind or hold them down. This kind of domination, the victory of the individual will over all obstacles and impediments, is Her special area of concern. In this way, like Mother Kali, She is directly responsible for the growth of human beings, dealing specifically with that area pertinent to challenges and obstacles. By frustrating the ill-intentioned hopes for domination in some and guiding those who sincerely strive for perfection, She fulfills an essential function in the impressive scheme of universal evolution.

X
Kamala

The tenth and final Mahavidya is the Mother of good fortune. As the very embodiment of positivity, standing radiantly at the end of the list, She represents the consummation of all that is positive in terrestrial and spiritual existence. Kamala has often been associated with Lakshmi, the Goddess of abundance, and is one of the names associated with Her. It is easy, then, to understand why all are attracted to Her, for She is the reward which occurs after the challenge has been met and victory has been secured. By bestowing boons of every kind and granting the quality of fearlessness, She brings life to its natural conclusion. Herein lies Her supreme secret.

Kamala is nothing less than the radiantly pure consciousness of the Atman, which is declared by the saints and sages to be of the very nature of unalloyed bliss. The conclusion of earthly life must inexorably lead to the land of immortality where all dualities are put to rest and the ups and downs of good and bad, virtue and vice, and pleasure and pain, are dissolved forever. The Goddess Kamala stands poised between these two worlds, bestowing freedom from one and entrance into the next. In this regard, She is Phalaharini Devi, the one who grants the fruit of all action and distributes just recompense were it is due. With characteristic joy She metes out the bountiful treasure of a divinely oriented life, granting the most priceless of attainments — immersion into Ultimate Reality. This indescribable condition is achieved by those whose earthly lessons have been well-learned, whose every karma has been destroyed, whose desire for individual existence has been effaced forever. What occurs thereafter is inexpressible, comprehendable only by direct perception. Goddess Kamala, Her face exuding the divine radiance of eternal happiness, opens the portals of transcendence and speeds souls along their way to the ultimate experience.

20

Karandamukuta:
Her Hairpiece Crown

The Gauge of True Freedom

The Universal Mother's mass of jet-black hair is taken up about Her head in a *Karandamukuta* — a hair-piece crown. This divine ornament is worn by Mother Durga and allows for both beauty of appearance and order. Symbolically, and since Her free-flowing hair suggests a spiritually emancipated condition, this would signify that the greatest freedom is only attained through careful control, that freedom is ever married to responsibility. This is one of the most elevated of teachings given to humanity and only those who are spiritually prepared and open-minded can accept and implement it into earthly and spiritual life.

One of the abiding tenets of freedom is well-illustrated by Sri Ramakrishna's story of the street musician. This public figure stands on busy corners or crowded byways and plays many instruments simultaneously, creating quite an amazing spectacle. He may hold a stringed instrument in one hand and a shaker or percussion instrument in the other. Strapped around his neck is a contraption that holds a wind instrument in place close to his mouth. His knees have two small cymbals strapped to them so he can provide rhythm while his foot controls a drumstick that beats out a meter against the drum sitting in front of him. Even amidst all these activities he manages to vocalize and imitate other instruments. All these things occur independent of one another yet with coordinated and harmonious results. The music that ensues, though orchestrated, is all produced by one individual. People stop and gawk, mesmerized and amazed by this phenomena.

This wonderful illustration could be used to express several different teachings, but in this context it explains well the necessity of control in order to achieve success and freedom. The Mother's Karandamukuta symbolizes this truth in a concise and clear manner. Freedom itself may be entirely unbounded, but the path leading to it requires the utmost discipline, just as the street musician's presentation required hours of practice and firm concentration. The lesson is obvious. For terrestrial beings, the need for the control of body, mind and all of life's activities is essential for peace of mind. Equanimity, abiding happiness and eternal contentment never come to those who are devoid of discipline. This is true for both worldly life and spiritual life which, when perfect and perpetual balance is attained, lose their respective and apparent distinctions and coalesce into one blissful experience. This, too, is illustrated by the Mother's shining crown. Both the flow of freedom represented by Her long black hair and the necessity of order and direction needed to experience it symbolized by the containing powers of the Karandamukuta are inseparable and fully dependent upon one another. One is direct experience, the other, that which makes it possible. The two articles and the qualities they epitomize contrast and complement each other simultaneously. This merging of opposites is one of the Mother's unique features.

Another lesson taught by the existence of the hairpiece crown is one of ultimacy. The infinite freedom represented by the flowing hair of the Universal Mother is overwhelming and needs some form to define its existence. The Karandamukuta is that structure, which gives shape, as it were, to the presence of a condition of emancipation that, like the Mother Herself, is both subtle and powerful. For aspiring beings, this distinction is all-important, for it aids the mind in the affirmation and realization of Her Supreme Intelligence. In this way, the crown fulfills the function of witness consciousness, without which any experience of freedom would remain an unknown condition, at least from the standpoint of relativity. All beings who are locked into the belief that individual awareness is real and who do not as yet possess the direct experience of the transcendent divinity abiding within them are heartened to know of this nondual condition. It makes sense out of all other aspects of the phenomenal universe. The lovely crown stands as a beacon then, radiating the light of a higher awareness to those still caught in the fundamental trap of duality.

Finally, the "crown at the crown" calls to mind the mystical presence of *Kundalini Shakti*. The Karandamukuta signifies the arrival of ascending consciousness at the spiritual center called the *Sahasrara Lotus,* the thousand-petaled vortex at the crown of the head. This final arrival takes place only after this subtle power has transfixed, transformed and transcended all six other lotuses located mystically within the subtle body associated with the spinal column. That the Universal Mother is wearing this brilliant symbol represents Her absolute mastery over the science of *Kundalini Yoga* and the total possession and control of its sublime force. The long flowing hair that issues from the crown's golden precincts infers that true freedom is gained only after the awakening and ascent of spirituality has reached the highest level and matured to the fullest extent.

The Karandamukuta is inset with an abundance of precious jewels. This indicates that all positive and valuable qualities abide eternally within the Divine Mother. These are not attributes which bind or limit the state of perpetual formlessness said to be the undying condition of ultimate Reality, nor are they simply ornaments by way of attainments or subtle powers. They represent the very nature of divine Reality, which by dint of Its infinity, contains all things within Its boundless expanse. Though Brahman is said to be attributeless, Its Shakti, ever one with Brahman, can take or select these powers or qualities and use them for dynamic expression. The formless Brahman and the ineffable Shakti — these "Two who are One" are also represented by the amazing phenomenon and appearance of the

Universal Mother's Karandamukuta. One is essential freedom from all impositions and the other, though free by nature at all times, creates and contains the concepts and structures of time, space, mind and the five elements, and sports blissfully through them.

21

Anklets and Bracelets of Snakes

Coils of Healing Protection

The lovely limbs of Mother Kali and Her divine consort, Lord Shiva, are adorned with snakes. Many Indian deities share this association with the reptile kingdom, including Lord Vishnu who rests on an entire bed of snakes while plunged in cosmic sleep. The *Nagas,* huge reptiles appearing repeatedly in the numerous stories contained in ancient Indian Mythology, are often extremely auspicious characters with many divine attributes. Some are Rishi-like in nature, graced with powers born of austerity. Others are possessed of refined and subtle intellects. Some find their place in *Itihasa* (cultural and spiritual history) as objects of great veneration, often associated with extremely important changes in history such as great wars, sacrifices and other noteworthy occurrences. Add to this the presence of spiritual power called *Kundalini,* represented iconographically by a coiled-up snake, and the meaning of these strange ornaments gracing Mother Kali's limbs becomes clearer.

The *Nagas* and *Naginis,* male and female reptile deities, represent powers inherent in the universe. Along with *Yakshas,* local gods and goddesses, and a whole host of other beings, they combine to manage and manipulate cosmic and terrestrial forces. Whereas the Yakshas are associated with the treasures of the kingdom such as minerals, gems and things born of the earth, and celestial deities preside over cosmic functions as they pertain to the three worlds, the Nagas and Naginis hold dominion over bodies of water such as lakes, streams, and oceans. Dwelling in these watery worlds, they thrive on and guard the life-energy abiding there. They also protect the aquatic beauty and the subaquatic treasures such as coral, pearls, seashells and underwater life. With regard to water itself, it is a healing element which not only fulfills the functions of quenching thirst and supporting life but is also used symbolically as a spiritual teaching to indicate the oneness and homogeneity of all existence. Its divine associations do not stop here but carry over into other pertinent matters. The fluid property of water forms the fundamental quality of every liquid, even ambrosial nectar, so its presence, whether in a pure or a mixed substance, is essential.

In this sense, the snakes which coil about the arms, legs and sometimes even the neck of Mother Kali, indicate the healing powers that She wields as She marches through the created worlds bestowing boons and allaying fears. The five elements, their subtle manifestations and the very powers which are inherent in them, pay homage to Her and lend their combined forces to Her service. With the earth's constituents and their subtle powers on Her side, there is no force that can resist Her supreme will. This is not surprising considering that She is the primal Creator, the *Adishakti,* the one on whom all seekers of the Truth rely.

In another sense, the reptile deities play an important role as well. The bed of snakes upon which Lord Vishnu reclines is actually one infinitely long reptile with many heads. This King of reptiles, called Ananta (infinite), or Shesha (literally, remainder or residue), represents the subtle essence of existence that remains after the earth and nether regions are all dissolved during *Pralaya* — universal dissolution. This representation emphasizes the unity of all existence. It also reveals the unlimited ability for manifestation that abides in a subtle state after dissolution and expresses Itself at the next cycle of creation.

In the Vishnu representation, Shesha, appearing as a backdrop of nine reptiles, indicates that divine Reality is at "rest," or in a static Self-absorbed condition. In the case of Mother Kali, these powers have been animated and are awake and fully functioning within the context of the universal play of consciousness. The dynamic *Mahashakti* is working Her magic deftly, complete with the superimpositions of the twenty-four cosmic principles of nature *(Prakriti)*, the three modes of existence *(gunas)* and the triune conceptual web of time, space and causality. Yet Brahman in equipoise as Ishvara can enter this inexplicable and tempestuous drama of manifestation without losing Its perfect balance. Utilizing action born of selflessness *(niskama karma)* which creates no residual effects in relativity, the *Avatar* or Divine Incarnation, enters the fray and becomes, as it were, the *Mahashakti* embodied.

That this perfect manifestation remains always attuned to ultimate Reality is instanced by the appearance of the royal reptile Ananta supporting the Avatar's descent, such as seen or heard about with regards to Lord Buddha's enlightenment. This protecting presence appeared on several occasions to shield the Divine Incarnation from danger in that age.

Another interesting and revealing feature about the Nagas and Naginis is the presence of a precious jewel within their heads. Bearing this valuable treasure is symbolic of awakened consciousness, the most prized possession of the saints and sages of every religious tradition. Plainly put, every being has as his or her essence the treasure of enlightened awareness, timeless, deathless and limitless. It is a matter of personal choice combined with divine Grace as to whether or not one discovers and unearths this priceless treasure in any given lifetime. Here as well, the subtle representatives of the reptile family act as aids. They are pictured in ancient stone reliefs at the portals of massive temples as guardians (dvara-pala) which regulate entrance into the sacred precincts of these shrines. This would indicate the importance of the necessity of taking initiation into a sacred path and entering into a regulated and prescribed spiritual practice.

The reference to Kundalini Shakti, often called "the serpent power," is obvious. The "coiled up" energy at the base of the spine, operating in a limited capacity among the first three centers of consciousness associated with evacuation, procreation and basic earthly sustenance and fulfillment, must be released to higher spheres at the heart, throat and third eye regions. The guardians of these spiritual portals, the Nagas and Naginis, are powers of the Divine Mother who wears them, as it were, around Her lovely limbs, the arms and legs being the seats of activity and accomplishment. Being conducted through these phases of spiritual growth by Her subtle internal forces, aspiring beings come to realize the divine nature of Reality and their own intrinsic connection with that Reality. As a snake wriggles easily through liquid waters, so too does the aspiring spiritual adept learn the conscious movements of transcending matter, ego, conceptual mind, and the universal laws while re-establishing a perfect and abiding identity with the Atman — the eternal, indwelling Self or Soul of all beings.

22
Demon and Jackal Companions

Negativity Unleashed upon Itself

Helpers of an entirely different nature, the demons and jackals accompanying Mother Kali, particularly on the stormy and terrible battlefield of relative existence, are perfectly suited to this terrain. Within the universal scheme of things and in keeping with the dual nature of the world where polar opposites clash interminably, these odd servants of the Mother provide a cold but necessary function. Often seen lapping up blood from dying victims or eating the flesh off of the dead bodies of fallen warriors, these strange beings symbolize the neutralization process penultimate to both the great dissolution and the resurrection of life.

In the realm of the mind, these beings represent the strong resolves that cause human beings to face the harsh realities surrounding the necessary purification process. The perfection of total transcendence, which occurs after universal dissolution, cannot abide with the presence of any activity or structure. Not even the memory of the carnage must remain! Only peace must reign supreme on that occasion, and the demons and jackals will see to it that the field of the mind is stripped bare of all thoughts, especially those negative tendencies which cause a return to relative existence. Thus are these weird companions truly Mother Kali's helpers, clearing the field of all impurities and recycling the contents.

On the field of battle, the ego must die. All sense of individuality must disappear, and with it all attachment to ephemeral structures and concepts. This must occur in order that transcendence of all limitations can be attained and the goal of human existence be reached. The Universal Mother has many ways of accomplishing the death of the ego. Sometimes, the most terrible and invincible foes have a weakness totally out of keeping with the strength they possess. This can be illustrated by the example of the full grown woman who is afraid of mice and spiders. The ego-enemy may have hidden fears that can bring about its downfall and demise. Knowing this, the Divine Mother sends Her considerable minions to effect this end. Not only jackals and demons make up this entourage, but rats, vultures, goblins, ghouls and other fantastic creatures also attend.

Somewhere in this march of terrible creatures exists the vehicle right for any particular job. Beholding the abundance of divine helpers of every name, size, shape, and form, beautiful and hideous as the situation requires, the ego finally expires under the force that most adequately epitomizes its greatest fear. With regards to the mind, this is seen as those thoughts, actions and aversions which cause us to react violently. These occurrences nearly always effect a revolution in human nature, for their stored up power, when unleashed, pricks the depths of the subconscious mind, the results of which appear as the emergence of passions, doubts, guilts and remorses which then finally see the light of day and get resolved. This part of the purification process is difficult and sometimes unbearable. The forces which instigate these often undesirable methods must be hard and merciless for the task at hand. This describes the well-chosen emissaries of the Divine Mother Kali perfectly. Since they thrive on negativity, inhabiting those realms of being where such things are commonplace, they prove to be adepts in such matters. The Universal Mother uses them in a fashion characteristic of Her; She always has a positive and beneficial end in view. Knowing this, Her children and votaries boldly face all challenges, surrendering to Her, relying fully upon Her and taking Her Name for the highest and best protection.

23

Lord Shiva Beneath Her Feet

The Flower and Its Fragrance

Encircling the delicate beauty of an island paradise, the liquid waves of a vast and infinite ocean bow repeatedly at its diminutive shores. Beholding the miniature perfection of his beloved newborn baby daughter, a full grown man weeps and pledges life-long adoration and service. Through examples such as these we may glean a little insight into the phenomena of Lord Shiva's awe and exaltation of the Universal Mother which has plunged Him into bliss merely upon glimpsing Her wondrous form. She is a spectacle of the most sublime variety, *"rare and thrilling to behold,"* as Ramprasad sings ecstatically and enthusiastically in one of his wisdom songs. Another famous song describes the union of Shiva and Mother Kali aptly:

> *Behold my Mother playing with Shiva,*
> *lost in an ecstasy of joy!*
> *Drunk with a draught of celestial wine,*
> *She reels, and yet She does not fall.*
> *Erect She stands on Shiva's bosom,*
> *and the earth trembles under Her tread;*
> *She and Her Lord are mad with frenzy,*
> *casting aside all fear and shame!*

About the thrilling vision of Mother Kali's earth-shaking dance, a contemporary poet exclaims:

The best that life can offer has combined with the most awe-inspiring terror that death is capable of and has assumed a form! Listen! She is of the densest black hue, but what I have seen has turned my hair white for all time! Her abundantly free-flowing locks of raven-colored hair are interminable periods of time, and all regions, divine, terrestrial or hellish, and the myriad forms that inhabit them are helplessly tied there forever, unable to get free! Across this infinite stretch of time and permeating it entirely, Her pervasive blackness reigns, infilling everything as space, both gross and subtle. Her fearsome yet enchanting laughter, rolling inexorably forth like peals of thunder, gives animating motion to all things. Her messengers and attendants, both sublime and terrifying, are entering the cosmic process to do Her bidding, operating a set of powerful laws that defy transcendence.

Yet there is a greater wonder than this, more subtle and endearing. Her momentary glance, falling here and there at perfect intervals, illumines and liberates embodied particles of Her consciousness from all bondage within that terrible web! What to speak of Her glance, Her bewitching smile lights up the three worlds and all attending regions with a radiance so beautiful that Truth Itself bows before Her. Millions of suns and stars, like tiny sparks burning in a black firmament, find at last an object worthy of worship and explode into Her darkness!

I can attest, my friend, that She is no ordinary divinity! Why else should the God of nondual wisdom have fallen at Her feet in speechless amazement! See, He swiftly loses normal consciousness, transported by what He has beheld! And what to wonder, for She has taken His very heart as Her personal abode, and dwells there in constant bliss, interminably. Rising from that precious realm, like fragrance from a flower, She fashions the perfect machine of creation, and instills it with life with Her own breath. Behold how She weaves into Her cosmic handicraft multiple twin strands of contrasting opposites, all bound together by the triple forces of nature. Her illusion is insurmountable, for She is the original authoress of creativity and destruction, primeval and eternal.

O Lord! I have seen Her sword of formless Truth flash with infallible accuracy, as by Her design the seas of birth and death swell. She purposefully topples the intricate machinery of manifestation that She created and dissolves all structures reminiscent of form! Countless human heads, centers of awareness free of all bodily attachments, are rolling towards Her Feet, smiles transfixing their faces, their disembodied voices chanting Her many victorious Names. Like marbles in a child's game, they obey some unseen force! Mountains of them are rising on all sides, and She stands astride, collecting them like grisly prizes. Rivers of blood from the carnage are pouring into Her open mouth as Her two eyes roll and Her protruding tongue dances here and there! All are returning to Her, are becoming absorbed by Her! All the while Her graceful hands are

calming fears and granting inconceivable boons!
The eye at the center of Her forehead is wide
open, but none can plumb its depths. Its timeless,
spaceless recesses exude an invisible nectar that
is palpable but unseen. Under its intoxicating
influence all beings are experiencing a transcen-
dent bliss that is indescribable. Excruciating fear
and all-attracting love are both dissolved in that
state, which destroys the very idea of division. In
the complete oneness of boundless peace, all
comes to rest at last in total unity and the primal
Goddess returns to Her own abode, the heart of
Shiva, as suddenly as She came, without warn-
ing! The "revered spiritual father" who describes
this awesome spectacle is no more than a child
before Her. Gazing through torrents of blissful
tears, he manages to articulate only a few sylla-
bles, chanting, 'Aum Ma, Aum Ma,' over and over
again.[20]

The classic description of the union of Shiva and
Shakti has been described in many ways and with
countless variations. These symbologies, though
incomprehensible to common people who remain
unawakened to all-pervasive Reality, are not
unknown to the devotees of the Divine Mother.
Fundamentally, Lord Shiva and His divine consort,
Mother Kali, both epitomize the embodiment of
nondual wisdom. This gets depicted through different modes which, though they are seemingly
opposite in orientation, are actually perfectly com-
patible, completely interchangeable and forever uni-

fied. In traditional representations, the great Lord Shiva stands for formless *Brahman,* the homogenous Reality that acts as a seamless backdrop against which the phenomena of relative existence get projected. Mother Kali, the original progenitress, is the author of the fantastic cosmic play *(Mahalila)* that streams forth from the heart of this Ultimate Reality. Both are one without a second, which is instanced by the fact that, as the Upanishads declare, both *Purusha,* the Supreme Soul and *Prakriti,* primal nature, are infinite, are without beginning or end.

Lord Shiva as Absolute Reality is not just an oversoul but is representative of *Ishvara,* the sum total of all souls and also the witness of the activities of gods and mankind. The Divine Mother Kali is not limited just to nature either, but plays Her part in the creation and direction of phenomenal existence in a perfectly detached manner. In all matters, the two share the same impersonal and detached manner, though one manages this through dynamic action and the other through static pervasiveness. In fact, the "Two who are One," as they are often called, are responsible for all that is known or will ever be known, being fully self-contained and the eternal source of the universe and what is beyond it. In the four comprehensible ways that God appears to us – as the Transcendental Supreme Being *(Param),* as the personal God or Creator *(Ishvara),* as the inner Self of all beings *(Atman or Antaryami)* and as the universal symbol *(Archa)* —

in all these ways are the Divine Couple, called *Shiva/Shakti*, found to exist, unified and complete, dancing and resting in turns while simultaneously coexisting in perfect harmony. The blend is so perfect as to mysteriously efface distinctions and separations completely, though apparent differences appear to exist. As matter emerges from and disappears into black holes in boundless space, so too do all dichotomies and dualities dissolve in this ecstatic and legendary union.

The "Two who are One" represent both the Ultimate Reality and the power to obscure it from comprehension. Absolute Reality represented by Lord Shiva is formless, with form and beyond both concepts as well. It is beyond name and form, is of the form of Its own nature and, as Sri Ramakrishna has stated, is much more that we cannot conceive of. The cosmic play, Mother Kali's domain, has these characteristics as well. It operates amidst name and form, utilizes the formless energy of prana and mentation, and is infinite in its scope and extremely subtle, possessing powers that can obscure Reality from view. Thus the Lord's Maya becomes manifest, creating a cosmic covering over what is eternally real, as if to veil that which can never be truly hidden. This is powerful manipulation on the level of the Divine Couple, which only They can understand. Such hypnotism fashions many *lokas* (worlds), intoxicates the gods and puts mankind into a sleep of ignorance bereft of true knowledge. This process proceeds through a kind of addiction to duality and a preoccupation with diversity. The state produced by desire and attachment of this type is truly a kind of sleep, and it gets facilitated through the wielding of the many diverse powers of Maya by the "Two who are One." Swami Vivekananda explains this essentially inscrutable process in poetic form:

> *O Thou most beautiful!*
> *Whose holy hands hold pleasure and hold pain!*
> *Doer of good! Who art Thou?*
> *The water of existence by Thee*
> *is whirled and tossed in mighty waves.*[21]

It appears that even Shiva falls into this hypnotic sleep, for He lies at the Cosmic Mother's Feet in supernal intoxication. However, it must be remembered that the poet stated that Shiva has lost *"normal consciousness."* He is not in an ordinary condition, but experiences a state of inward absorption into Absolute Reality, brought about by the vision of an externalized version of the eternal principle. The Ultimate has taken a form in this case, and the sight of this divine manifestation, whose beauty is beyond compare, transports the lover of Truth into ecstasy. Premdas, the ecstatic poet, expresses Her loveliness in a song:

> *Upon the sea of the world*
> *unfolds the lotus of the New Day, and there*
> *the Mother sits enshrined in blissful majesty.*
> *See how the bees are mad with joy,*

sipping the nectar there.
Behold the Mother's radiant face, which so
enchants the heart and captivates the universe!
About Her Lotus Feet bands of ecstatic holy men
are dancing in delight.
What matchless loveliness is Hers,
what infinite pervades the heart when She appears!
O brothers and sisters, says Premdas,
I humbly beg you, one and all,
to sing the Mother's praise.[22]

Even a momentary appearance of this essence of
all forms is enough to transform normal consciousness, for Her riveting dance of victory destroys all
other considerations and focuses the mind solely
upon Truth. Though the Divine Mother Kali dances
madly into the realms of space and time that She so
adeptly creates, She never loses Her balance or forgets Her purpose. Hers is a dance that integrates
perfect composition with freedom and spontaneity.
She is amazing to behold, a vision seen only by
those who have transcended attachment to the idea
of relativity. Her dance is without a false step and
demonstrates both inherent perfection and perfect
equipoise. These endearing qualities are well-
expressed in a poem by Swami Vivekananda:

To friend and foe Thy lotus-eyes are even;
Ever Thine animating touch brings fruit
to fortunate and unfortunate alike;
The shade of death, and immortality —
both these, O Mother, are Thy grace Supreme!

*Mother Supreme! Oh, May Thy gracious face
never be turned away from me, Thy child!*[23]

This pervasive equanimity, so subtle as to be
invisible and practically indiscernible, is the secret
to the Divine Couple's eternal embrace of unified
ecstasy. The simple truth is that only oneness
exists, despite all seeming alterations and modifications brought about by diverse manifestation. The
very condition of diversity is supported and permeated by oneness. The ignorant get seduced by the
many appearances while the wise remain cognizant
of the one abiding presence. In short, the former
dream the dreams of duality and fall into the fundamental sleep of delusion while the latter abide in
nondual Reality, exalting in eternal union. The
Mahanarayana Upanishad explains the essence of
the secret of the "Two who are One":

*This universe is truly the Divine Being only.
Therefore it subsists on That — the Self-Effulgent
Divine Being — who has many heads and many
eyes, who is the producer of joy for the universe,
who exists in the form of the universe, who is the
master and cause of humanity, whose forms are
the various gods, who is imperishable, who is the
all-surpassing ruler and savior, who is superior to
the world, who is endless and omniform, who is
the goal of humanity, who is the destroyer of sin
and ignorance, who is the protector of the universe and the ruler of individual souls, who is
permanent, supremely auspicious and unchanging,*

who is embodied in mankind as its support, who is supremely worthy of being known by the creatures, who is embodied in the universe and is the supreme goal.

This explanation of the One in the many, sometimes called unity in diversity, is typical of the wisdom contained in the Vedas and Upanishads. It is at the root of the Vedanta Philosophy and is the only healing balm for the problems of life. Through teachings such as these we are able to realize that the Supreme Being is not far away from us in some distant region, perched on a cloud or abiding in an unattainable heaven, but is immediate and all-pervasive, present in every moment and fully accessible. Lord Shiva does not sleep, but keeps constant vigil. His continuing vision of Mother Kali, whether it be of Her externalized form or Her subtler Reality, is nothing less than perfect omniscience. When witnessing Her dance, He is blessing the creation with His purifying attention and when He is plunged into *samadhi* due to Her inconceivable sublimity, He is fortifying the very foundations of Reality with His spiritual insight. One mode is Grace, the other is transcendence, and both are needed. Mother Kali signals this truth with Her two hands, poised in symbolic positions. The *Varada Mudra,* which dispenses boons, indicates Her Grace flowing to all creatures, while Her *Abhaya Mudra,* the assurance of fearlessness, inspires all to transcendent realization. It has been mentioned that Lord Shiva and Mother Kali are interchangeable in their respective functions. The Divine Couple is always and ever unlimited. What one represents, the other can adeptly facilitate. This is understood through an exploration of sacred mythology, for both the *Shrutis* (the Vedas and Upanishads) and the auxiliary texts (the Epics, *Smritis, Puranas* and *Tantras*) taken together, form a comprehensive picture. Lord Shiva, for instance, represents Supreme Reality while lying at Mother Kali's lotus feet, but in the embodied condition and while making His way about the three worlds, He disseminates wisdom, marries, has a family and practices austerities for the good of mankind and to hone His own ongoing realization. Both modes, the personal and transpersonal, are seen to be equally comfortable for Him.

Such is the case with Mother Kali as well. She can clothe Herself in the garb of a Warrior Goddess and appear on the battlefield of relativity, or plunge Herself into a formless condition and become *Digambari,* clad in space, with transcendence as Her only vesture. Therefore, when one mode of Divine expression is present, the other is naturally inferred. *Shiva* is never without *Shakti*, for fire is never without its power to burn. *Shakti* is always one with *Shiva,* for a fragrance needs the flower from which to emanate. This "Ever One" condition, if understood properly, puts to rest all manner of doubt and dissension. For example, the futile struggle for supremacy between those who pose Divine Reality to be either feminine or masculine is undermined completely, for the transcendental Soul of the

Universe is beyond gender. Seen from another standpoint, the femininity of Lord Shiva emerges in His sensitivity for all suffering beings, while the masculine nature of Mother Kali is demonstrated in no uncertain terms through Her heroic acts of battle against the demonic forces that threaten Her precious spiritual children. Here again, the interchangeable nature of the "Two who are One" becomes apparent. To forget this secret of inseparable oneness or fail to maintained it as the essence of one's understanding, allows the mind to fall repeatedly into the fundamental error of dual thinking.

In the consummate spiritual experience, the tenor of which has plunged Lord Shiva into a profound condition, nothing is missing, nothing is left out, for there is no need for exclusion of any type. The intense spiritual state that all beings seek, which is the very essence of their true nature, is all-encompassing. The *neti, neti* phase of spiritual struggle has matured into the *iti, iti*[24] state of perfect acceptance. Even the penultimate level of self-surrender is over. All that is left is a natural spontaneity blended with an exquisite spiritual sensitivity, itself the very epitome of internal purity. In a way, it is no wonder that Lord Shiva has fallen into a spiritual swoon, for He has seen the Wisdom Mother, in all Her awesome glory, dance before Him. This spiritual sensitivity can become so subtle that, as was the case with Sri Ramakrishna Paramahamsa, the slightest suggestion of anything sacred — a devotional song, a picture of the Himalayas, a broom made with materials found only in the birthplace of Lord Chaitanya — was enough to drown Him almost irretrievably in an ocean of spiritual bliss! This happened repeatedly. His life was filled constantly with a multitude of sublime experiences.

Thus it is that Lord Shiva teaches us a valuable lesson about religious life and the precious experiences that are so rare of occurrence. All who would immerse themselves in this sublime realm and breathe the rarefied atmosphere of unconditional love and nondual wisdom must become extremely pure and ultra-sensitive to matters of the Spirit. The intensification of *sadhana* through austerities and renunciation culminates in an almost effortless one-pointedness that leaves the devotee naturally inclined towards spiritual life. At this level of advanced practice, where the practitioner becomes the adept, spiritual struggle matures into joyful preoccupation. From this lofty plateau, where action and inaction merge into the subtle balance of perfect equanimity, the "practice" of constant abidance in the Self is all that is left. This condition places the purified mind into an entirely receptive mode where all phenomena and experiences are permeated with the presence of the Divine. Imagine then, the depth of insight and the intensity of feeling present in the mind of Lord Shiva upon witnessing the "Dance of the Noumenon," the intricate and multifarious movements of the Supreme Enchantress who is the beloved Mother of the Universe!

24

Her Cosmic Dance

The Cosmic Choreographer

"An expert dancer never takes a wrong step!" This remark by Sri Ramakrishna is meant to convey the sense of total surrender to God under which the true devotee operates and an idea of the complete and perfect refuge granted to those who are capable of making the supreme sacrifice of offering the entire being — life, mind, heart, body and senses — to the Divine Mother of the Universe. If such an offering is made in the proper spirit, consciously and wholeheartedly, the blessed Lord and Divine Mother assumes all responsibility for the devotee. What follows is an end to all suffering, an abiding knowledge of the *Atman* and total absorption into the highest ideal. In short, this amounts to the attainment of the goal for human existence.

Mother Kali's cosmic dance has an infinite set of movements. It is filled with both intricate subtleties and grand designs. On the subtle level, She choreographs Her masterpiece from many unseen elements at Her disposal, those being such exquisite functions as time, space, causality, thought, sound, and intelligence. The external components of Her dance comprise an infinite and complex series of interactions using matter and energy. The five elements, the physical bodies of living beings and the life-force that She animates them with, all form a part of the universal segment of Her dance. Creation, preservation and destruction are the phases of this stunning composition while activity, inertia and balance weave it all together.

A dance must have motion, must have symmetry, must express what is in the heart and must be possessed of both composition and spontaneity. What is more, to truly warrant its place as an art form, it must have meaning, and it should convey this meaning to all who stand as witnesses to it. Mother Kali's dance is the infallible movement of the Divine Being. Its symmetry lies in the fact that it draws together every element in existence (the twenty-four *Tattvas*) and weaves them into a fitting background over which life itself can be acted out. What to speak of heartfelt expression, the Universal Mother's cosmic dance is love incarnate, enacted out of sheer compassion and performed solely for the sake of love. The substance of Her dance is created from the triple principles of omniscience, omnipresence and omnipotence, and spontaneity itself has been captured forever in Her every thought and movement.

Some limited thinkers have speculated that the cosmos, the Divine Mother's created playground, is bereft of any logical sequence and that Her play or dance, the *Mahalila,* is sporadic and haphazard, based upon coincidence. They say that even if there is a Universal Mother who creates, that She must be a mad woman, bereft of normal sensibility or intoxicated beyond reason. Who else could manifest such a chaotic universe? These so-called thinkers commit a primal error. They draw up their conclusions regarding the Divine Being based upon the limited capacity of their own minds. Their comprehension of God is fashioned under the same restrictions that are applicable to human beings.

The Supreme Being, however, is beyond all such limitations and transcends even the sharpest intellect. Otherwise, how could such a Being manifest this boundless universe which is itself infinite and beyond the mind's ability to fathom? Therefore, the primal error committed by human beings in this area consists of applying limited human characteristics to the Supreme Being. In both religion and philosophy, this amounts to the most narrow type of dualism.

Dualism, in the way that it is usually understood, is predicated upon the existence of two or many. If there is a creation present, if there are many gods in vogue, if there is more than one "Reality" vying for supremacy, that is taken to be a dualistic state. When a powerful manifestation of God is present, however, like the advent of an Avatar, the nature of dualism gets truly revealed. Dualism, placed under the spotlight of Truth, is simply the acceptance of diversity or multiplicity as Reality. In short, duality is illusion, or Maya. There is really no such thing as duality, there is only Oneness. The One pervades the many, and the many exist solely in the One.

Applying this simple truth to the fundamental error of human misconception, we can examine the manifestation of the universe and the Divine Creator in an entirely different light. With regards to the universe, all objects appearing there are composed of the same materials. Trees, flowers and other plant life consist of the same elements, bodies of water possess the same properties, even the physical frames of human beings are of one blood and one flesh. Thought and life-force are shared commonly by all and even the oxygen we breathe is one and the same. Similarly, in the realm of spirituality, all gods and goddesses represent so many expressions of the same Reality. Everywhere one turns — in all directions — as well as inward and outward, there exists only unity, eternal and indivisible. This ineffable and inseparable Reality, when comprehended to any extent, dissolves all notions of dualism. It is, as Lord Krishna often says, *"the string which connects the pearls together."* To quote Holy Mother, Sri Sarada Devi:

> *Everything comes into existence in time and disappears in time. Deities and such things really disappear at the dawn of enlightenment. The aspirant then realizes that the Mother alone pervades the entire universe. All then become one. This is the simple Truth.*[25]

The Mother that pervades the universe, then, is not limited to form. How could a limited form pervade anything? Relegating Her to a human or celestial image alone is a major mistake — a "primal error." To know Her as formless essence first and foremost is to open the doors of subtle insight. From this vantage point it is easy to comprehend how Her essence as pure conscious Awareness infills everything: how She becomes the subtle energy which animates life; how She manifests as the ethers which support all forms, as air filling the lungs, as fire lighting and warming the universe, as the cleansing waters and the solid earth. It is evident how She operates the laws of gravity and motion to maintain order in the universe, and how She enters and dwells within the minds of the enlightened as intelligence. The obvious truth about Her all-pervasive presence becomes clear when She is seen to abide in the hearts and minds of all beings as various qualities such as love, kindness, compassion, patience and other virtues. Truly, She is everywhere, and any conception of the Divine Mother which is devoid of the truth of this eternal and pervasive unity is distorted and incomplete at best. It will only serve to foster the illusion of duality and cause painful rifts and separations in life and delusion in the minds of living beings.

For those who are not yet familiar or comfortable with the Universal Mother's omnipresence, certain teachings are given. Faith, trust and devotion to God are sterling qualities but they are hard of attainment. To illustrate the infallible nature and the perfect workings of the Divine Mother of the Universe, Sri Ramakrishna transmitted spiritual teachings through devotional wisdom songs. A pertinent line in one such song that He was particularly fond of singing reveals the Universal Mother to be a harmonious blend of practical efficiency and ecstatic bliss. The Great Master would sing, *"Drunk with a draught of celestial wine, She reels, and yet She does not fall."* As is indicated, the Divine Mother is always experiencing pure joy, whether She is dancing in a manifest state or abiding as formless Reality. While expressing the infinite potential of the Absolute through finite forms, She becomes mad with bliss, but She never forgets Her sacred duty to all created structures and always oversees every aspect of the creation with the utmost care. She is the essence of all divine qualities. Since this is the case, attributes such as wisdom, omniscience and perfection constitute integral parts of Her being. How can the Mother of nondual Truth, whose wisdom is the mainstay of all saints and sages, who oversees, manages and protects the multifarious affairs of this vast creation, who is the chosen ideal for the gods and the Avatars — how can Her actions and intentions ever run counter with the attainment of the highest good? Therefore, to find the true meaning of Mother Kali's phenomenal dance, accomplished with perfect balance, it is necessary to follow the trail that She Herself clears and treads in every age, a path which bears Her name, the way of Goddess Kali — the Wisdom Mother.

With regards to the purpose for Her cosmic dance — why the creative power should produce such a world of diverse manifestation — this is a difficult question to answer. The reason the Divine Mother loves to dance, why She creates, where She gets Her resources and how She puts it all together and maintains it — these are questions that receive no satisfying answer, especially for the mind posited in relativity. "Her sweet will," is as good an answer as any, for She is extremely self-willed, being the highest Self of all beings and having their highest good in mind at all times. Being the Mother of all mothers and epitomizing the essence of all maternal qualities, She is supremely suited to manage the affairs of the creation She has so deftly fashioned, including the birth, preservation and dissolution of each and every created structure in the three worlds. Therefore, putting such ultimately futile questions aside, it is useful to simply study what is known about Her and Her timely and auspicious methods. Deeper insight will thereby gradually dawn on the mind. As Ramprasad, a devotee of the Divine Mother often sings,

"Strive intensely to comprehend the Universal Mother.
You will never be able to know Her
but your mind will be purified in the attempt."

Her Dance as Superimposition

The Universal Mother, dancing throughout space and time, possesses an infinite set of moods and demonstrates an endless series of movements. She rivets the minds of all beings upon relative existence, bewitching and enchanting apparently individualized consciousness in millions of different ways. To know Her as the Mistress of the cosmic dance is to be swept up in ecstasy, like Lord Shiva. To forget Her, however, is to be swept away in confusion and ignorance.

As wonderful as this ecstasy is, it is also rare. To look realistically at the world is to become aware of the all-pervasive suffering that permeates existence. A downward fall into the sleep of delusion is accompanied by a misery no less intense than the experience of bliss in a positive mode. This tendency towards forgetfulness, then, is the cause of most of the grief and suffering experienced in the creation. The rest is woven into the very fabric of relativity by design in the form of contrasting opposites such as pleasure and pain, good and evil, life and death, etc. Thus, present in the cosmic process, there is an individual ignorance as well as a collective or universal delusion. These two, working in tandem, help form the makeup of what Vedanta teachers call "false superimposition" over Reality.

An analysis of the creation, the act of discrimination (*Viveka*) which brings all aspects of it into focus, reveals both the nature of relativity and a way of escape from it. Given that the Divine Mother is the fundamental power in the universe, the *Adishakti*, and understanding that Her will is supreme, gives rise to a beneficial act of self-surrender. Most beings see no efficacy for it due to the presence of ignorance in their minds. Pseudo-spiritual beings talk glibly about self-surrender but fail miserably in its attainment. It is the penultimate stage of realization and its accomplishment cannot be feigned. Wishful thinking, fantasizing, pretending and even surface affirmation — these are a few of the techniques used to try to win this prize. In the end, as is the case with most valuable attributes, it takes commitment, hard work and constancy to be successful, and these are not possible without devotion to the ideal and a strong desire to attain it. Mind and heart must work together, then, to secure this priceless spiritual treasure.

As discrimination matures, the intellect gets honed to a fine point and is able to penetrate into any problem and discover the proper and adequate solution. With regards to the difficult dance of life, the devotee discovers that the individual ignorance present in the mind can be destroyed or transcended. It also becomes clear, though, that the grand design of the Mother's cosmic dance is impossible to change, and that all beings must bear with and accept its apparent imperfections. In short, personal delusion, one's own ignorance, can be overcome. False superimposition over Reality on the universal level, however, must be perceived as an intended obscuration placed there by the supreme and inscrutable will of the Divine Mother. Only She and those She chooses to enlighten are aware of the reasons for its existence. Armed with this knowledge, taking care of personal concerns and leaving the operation of the universe to the Divine Mother, the devotee continues to practice an intense and ongoing sadhana for the purification of the body/mind mechanism. This resolute divine act triggers a unique occurrence. The mind and intellect, purified by individual effort combined with knowledge, now becomes fit for receiving the Grace of the Supreme Being. It is this descent of sublime attention from the Universal Mother that allows for the transcendence of the world and all its limitations.

False superimposition is often described in

terms of coverings or sheaths, called *koshas* and *upadhis* in Sanskrit, which veil Reality from view. For example, on the microcosmic or individual level, the body is one covering. Its material nature and transitory condition make it fit only for the temporary housing of consciousness. Delusion regarding its ephemeral nature, though, causes limited awareness to associate with it and cherish it as if it were eternal. Thus it becomes an impediment towards realizing that which is truly lasting and substantial. It is important to note that ignorance is of the mind. Those who know the embodied condition to be transitory, see the body as a temple for the holy Spirit. Remaining aware of its limitations, they focus on the mind which is the seat of all delusion, for the mental sheath transmigrates after death while the physical one does not. Since this is the obvious fact, the enlightened give only so much attention to the body as will be conducive for its bare maintenance. When illumination dawns on the purified mind, body consciousness naturally diminishes. This is an example of the natural transcendence of a limiting sheath.

While studying a holy personage, it is seen that the mind of that being is quite free from egotism. The ego is another sheath, that part of the mental complex which, when not refined or controlled, causes selfish preoccupation with individual existence. Its refinement is essential, for in its immature state it represents a very thick covering over Reality. Light of a universal nature, true wisdom, cannot penetrate the ego of an unawakened person, who remains impervious to knowledge and Truth. Self-surrender, devotion to the Lord and other conscious offerings allow for the transcendence of this superimposition and return the mind to its original pristine state. The mind itself, and even that aspect of it called the intellect, are sheaths which veil higher Reality. Everyone is aware of the limitations of the mind. Even so, its potential must be tapped and realized. This happens in the sheath of the intellect, which, when illumined, is the most subtle and responsive property of the human condition. It responds to spiritual truths when, through practices which lead to realization, it becomes calm, deep and translucent and merges with Absolute Reality. This is the "no mind" state spoken of in the nondual philosophies of all true religions.

Other sheaths associated with the individual are also present. All of them are used by the Universal Mother to express some aspect of the creation. Thus, Her dance continues at every level. Since individual beings are expressions of the Absolute, they possess consciousness. This sentiency is a unique characteristic which separates them from insentient matter. Both evolve, and both have the Atman as the ground for their existence, but sentient beings possess awareness, can think and act of their own volition. This is why the Mother's dance, on the microcosmic level of the individual, has such intense meaning. Much more is at stake, as it were, for there is great potential present due to the abidance of a living, aspiring consciousness. The cosmic aspect of Her dance, being a manifestation of Her great power, is more grandiose and awe-inspiring, involving sets of laws placed in motion to provide a material backdrop over which the evolution of sentient beings can take place.

On a macrocosmic level, the universe and its constituents (the 24 *Tattvas* — Cosmic Principles) are viewed as a superimposition over Reality. Like clouds which hide the sun, the universe, its many aspects, the maze of time, space and causality all obscure the Light of Truth. Even the very power which projects the universe, called *Mahamaya,* is deemed a power of enchantment which causes Reality to appear as something unreal and causes that which has no true substance to appear real. Therefore, illusion and subtle trickery are inherent in the very fabric of relativity. Creation, preservation and destruction all demonstrate, over and over again, the noneternal nature of manifest names and forms, whether they be tiny like the atom or as vast as a universe.

To illustrate the nature of illusion and its resultant delusion, the example of the adept human dancer is helpful. The intricate movements, techniques and visuals which she utilizes both hypnotizes and enthralls the viewer, often creating illusory appearances. As a result, the dancer appears to be actually flying, feet never touching the earth, or seems to have become so fluid that the form melts into one moving stream, inhabiting all of space simultaneously. If these tricks of the senses are produced by a mere physical body in motion, imagine the enchantment that the Universal Dancer Herself is capable of producing! Such marvelous bewitchment gives entirely new meaning to the words deception and enchantment.

Indeed, most beings are thoroughly deceived by this universal display that the Divine Mother presents. This is, as Vedanta says, "taking the unreal for the Real." As a snake charmer hypnotizes the cobra with repetitive motion and tantalizing sound, so does the elemental dance of creation, preservation and destruction seize the consciousness of living beings. With the mind's awareness fastened upon the seductive principles of nature — the five elements, body, life-force, mind, ego and senses, beings move in rhythm to external stimulus, scarcely noticing the inner primal essence which is static, immutable and eternal. What is more, this essence is blissful by nature, possessed of an intoxication that is the Divine Mother's own limitless ecstasy, proceeding, in part, from Her transcendent joy of the creative process.

This divine elixir is free of the impurities of the elemental dance. It does not bring the sickness of egotism, desire, attachment, aversion and the like, nor does it produce the indigestion of anger, lust, greed, jealousy and covetousness. It is not moving one instant and stagnant the next, nor is it alive one moment and dead thereafter. A taste of this delightful ambrosia causes the layers of superimposition to fall away, unveiling the Truth and revealing one's true nature to be eternal and indivisible. The experience does not end here either! The Universal

Mother dances on, creating ever-new and fresh expressions. Not only is the abiding perfection of the individual Self revealed, but the entire cosmos now takes on the attributes of divinity, showing itself to be nothing less than a single Reality in so many forms. As the Mother's dance intensifies, forms begin to evaporate. The entire universe then disappears and only the ineffable light of pure Consciousness remains. Pure Consciousness is the eternal substratum, present at the beginning, abiding throughout, and remaining after all is dissolved.

Herein lies the secret of the Divine Mother's dance. It is an eternal celebration of form and formlessness, and that which provides the consistency and cohesiveness for both of these modes to exist and interact. In terms of manifestation, She dances and rests in turns, but that which is ever present during activity and inactivity, during the modes of motion and stillness, during periods of form and formlessness, that is Her especial love, and She dances perfectly and untiringly so as to attract all beings to It. Those who follow are the true knowers, the masterful dancers who transcend life and death.

Others, those who are left behind, choose a world of attachment to changing names and forms, drinking a broth which, though it may taste sweet initially, turns bitter in the end. As Sri Krishna states in the *Bhagavad Gita,* being completely sensitive to the highest good of his devotee, Arjuna,

That which is like poison at first,
but like nectar at the end;

that happiness is said to be Sattvika,
born of the translucence of the intellect
due to Self-realization.
That happiness which arises from the contact
of the senses and their objects
and which is like nectar at first
but like poison at the end —
it is held to be Rajasika.
That happiness which deludes the self both
at the beginning and at the end and which arises
from sleep, sloth, and miscomprehension —
that is declared to be Tamasika.

These three modes, the triple *gunas*, defined as balance, activity, and inertia, permeate every aspect of life. In a state of delusion, the gunas of *rajas* and *tamas,* in accordance with the ignorant mind, are responsible for distortions of all types. Two of the most obstinate areas of mundane human existence, relationships and addictions, both born of and complicated by desire and attachment, recur in countless permutations and seldom find resolution. As a result, peace of mind, so important to spiritual evolution, is rarely attained to any substantial degree. Illumined beings speak to both of these problems, offering timely warnings and beneficial advice. About the tricky arena of human relationships, Ramprasad, the experienced lover of God, sings: *"The passionate words of a selfish lover may first taste sweeter than honey, but they contain the poison of delusion."*[26] There are many suffering beings who can easily relate to the poet's pithy words, but as the

Great Master, Sri Ramakrishna, has stated, "*The camel loves to eat thorny bushes, and continues even though its gums hurt and bleed profusely.*"

This area of the Mother's dance reveals the presence of the six passions, which are additional obscurations that hide Truth and Reality from view. Indulgence in these six areas brings pain and pleasure in turn, which always ends in suffering. Humanity, in every age and at every location, seeks satisfaction of the passions which breed obsessions that last for lifetimes. In contemporary times, one such obsession is evident in the area of addiction to external intoxicants. Sri Ramakrishna, noting the deluded and fanciful state of mind possessed by those under the influence of external intoxicants, stated simply and profoundly: "*The hemp smoker believes that his inebriation is a form of spiritual ecstasy. But it is nothing of the kind. He deludes himself in his indolence into such a belief.*" Such delusion is widespread among those who have no idea of the true and lasting condition of inner bliss which arises from spiritual life. For the truly illumined, the only addiction present in them is to Truth, for authentic freedom proceeds from It.

The paths of light and darkness are choices left to the discretion of individuals, those embodied in a human form. These two paths outline the difference between a life of boundless freedom and a life of stale repetition. One form of Mother's dance uplifts and liberates while the other leads to deeper entrenchment and greater bondage. The presence of *Maya,* and its ability to obscure Truth and the pathways leading to spiritual emancipation, is enough to delude the minds of most human beings, causing them to cherish matter rather than worship Spirit. As Ramprasad sings poignantly, *"Floating in the Cosmic Mother's womb, we are all contemplatives, but once we take birth in the world of separation, we consume earth instead of nectar."*[27] This is the most unfortunate condition in the universe, far worse than poverty, disease, famine or other catastrophes, because lack of the awareness of one's true nature is poverty, hunger and illness of the worst variety. It represents the loss of absolute perfection, inherent holiness, everlasting sanctity and eternal peace of mind. The loss of spiritual Consciousness is really the reason for the presence of suffering on all levels of existence, for if God were realized within and all around, all such calamities would disappear, both from earthly life and from spiritual life.

For those whose spiritual efforts and aspirations take them to the portal of a divine life, an abundance of sublime realizations and precious boons await. Spiritual emancipation is accompanied by a host of blessings, not the least of which is holy communion with the Supreme Being — the source and origin of the universe. It is here that the true meaning for the Divine Mother's cosmic dance begins to be comprehended, and all the burning questions that plague the minds of struggling beings get answered in turn. This represents the meaning and purpose of life and leads, as well, to its consummation and fulfillment.

Her Dance as Fulfillment

A dance always has benefits, both for the artist and for the audience. The fruits which proceed from Mother Kali's enriching dance have been described by the sages as the *Purushartas*, or the Four Fruits of Life. These are well-known as *Dharma*, conscious and righteous living, *Artha*, right livelihood, *Kama*, the satisfaction of legitimate desires, and *Moksha*, liberation from all limitation, often called spiritual emancipation. The order in which these are placed is of extreme importance. *Dharma*, righteous living in a consciously aware state of being, sets the stage for both protection from danger and proper utilization of what is to come. Without a moral and ethical foundation based upon spiritual sensitivity, without the knowledge of one's inherent destiny and direction and a path to follow in the fulfillment of that *dharma*, the fruits which follow can turn rotten and even poisonous. This is easily understood by witnessing the condition of worldly people.

Artha, usually defined as the acquisition of worldly goods for one's own prosperity and happiness, and *Kama*, the satisfaction of desires, are fruits which get bestowed upon all living beings. This fact is often puzzling to sincere seekers, who see that wealth and the satisfaction of desires are enjoyed equally in this life by persons of both moral and immoral character. A single life, however, a blink of the eye of the creator, is a short time span in which to judge the inexorable laws of karma, which confer just retribution for all actions committed in life, whether they be positive or negative. A portion of the Divine Mother's dance is taken up with this incomprehensible field of activity.

Certainly, embodied beings can have as much of wealth and sensual satisfaction as they desire, for the Universal Mother is the *Kalpataru,* the wish-fulfilling tree that grants all wishes and desires. All should be careful, however, for what they ask! To borrow a fitting analogy, one, two or even three chocolate cupcakes is a great delight to a young boy, but if he is forced to eat a dozen or more, each additional one beyond the limit of enjoyment results in exquisite torture! Such is the case with more subtle enjoyments as well, but the danger here is not just physical discomfort but karmic repercussion resulting in bondage and delusion. The dance, at this point, is accompanied by music that is out of tune and discordant! Creating an ever-increasing web of deceit full of mundane habits, hypocritical justifications and subtle deceptions, and wallowing in a limited and paltry life of materiality based upon the senses alone, the *adharmic* person not only experiences greater suffering in direct proportion to greater enjoyment, but relegates the vastly superior life of spirituality to an inferior position, forgetting the true Self in the process.

This depressing and hopeless condition never occurs to one in possession of a *dharmic* disposition. Taking only enough to satisfy basic living requirements and fulfilling only those desires which arise as a natural result of daily living in a sacred environment, the contented spiritual aspirant lives a simple and carefree existence, free of the ponderous weights of inordinate wealth and pressing desires. If vast wealth comes as a matter of course, being decreed by the Divine Mother of the Universe Herself, it gets used for the good of religious pursuits and to benefit others. If all the desires of life surface and cry out for fulfillment, the very purity of a dharma-oriented nature places them all in perspective and an aspirant methodically derives ultimate satisfaction from them in turn. Whereas the desires of an *adharmic* person act like gasoline poured on a fire, causing it to burn higher and higher, the desires of the *dharmic* person are like wood, which after providing warmth and utility, turn to ashes and disappear forever. Fulfillment resulting in freedom is the outcome for those who implement *dharmic* living as the foundation for their life, perceiving its importance as superior to both wealth and worldly satisfaction.

As the Divine Mother's dance becomes more and more refined, attuning itself to the subtler nature of spiritual life, the fourth fruit called *Moksha,* or liberation, is attained. There is a distinction between mere salvation and spiritual emancipation. Those whose spiritual power is as yet undeveloped, and who must rely upon external aid from the Divine Mother's many helpers, attain to salvation and continue on in their course towards total freedom, which all are seeking, either knowingly or unknowingly. Others, comprehending the significance of Self-knowledge and turning their loving attentions

towards the Supreme Being, seek to see through the
very fabric of relativity that creates the illusory
nature of manifestation. Piercing through the veils
of Maya, the superimposition of all coverings over
the Ultimate Reality, they unite with That and transcend the necessity of rebirth forever.

In a general sense, the various types of liberation
have distinctions according to attainment and can
be classed for study and analysis. First of all, there
is *Videha Mukti,* which is a freedom from all types of
embodied existence. In this case, the Self, which
knows itself to be pure Consciousness, seeks a
higher expression and immerses itself in the formless ocean of conscious Light. Videha Mukti does
not mean that embodied existence will never occur
again, but that the embodied condition will not be a
forced situation due to karmic propensities. Sri
Ramakrishna used the analogy of the mongoose
kept captive by children. In order to keep it as a
pet, they tie a brick to its tail so that it will be unable
to climb the wall to its hole. The inexorable weight
of the brick causes it to fall down again and again,
despite repeated efforts to ascend. The stored up
and unresolved karma of an unillumined being acts
in this way, bringing about repeated births and
deaths on the wheel of *samsara,* deluded existence.

Patanjali, the father of Yoga and author of the
Patanjala Yoga Sutras, describes the videha-muktis
and the prakriti-layas as those who escape physical
rebirth for a time, but due to their inability to transcend unmanifest prakriti, subtle realms of expression, create many universes and lord over them for

long periods of time. Their attachment to bliss in this regard and their fear of dissolution which brings an end to such limited pursuits and pleasures, causes them to fall again into the realm of birth and death. Therefore, the idea of Videha Mukti has several distinctions. Whereas the being possessed of Videha Mukti is more likely to rush towards final liberation, being drawn irresistibly, the *jivanmukta* is of a stature that has realized the one pure Consciousness existing everywhere, at all times. In the state of *jivanmukti*, enlightenment is an eternal verity that is impervious to all superimpositions, including the notions of embodiment or disembodiment. In this condition, the illumined being is liberated under all circumstances, never forgetting the true nature of Reality. This is a rare and precious boon, only bestowed upon those who have important matters to fulfill in the Universal Mother's work. Such as these are the spiritual teachers of mankind whose duty it is to work in the fields and reap a harvest of enlightened beings. The jivanmuktas perceive the inner meaning behind the creation, thus revealing for others those precious moments of genius and synchronicity in the Mother's cosmic dance.

There are other levels of liberation, but at the top of the list is the consummate state of being called *Sarva Mukti*. As its name infers, it is "all liberation." There are no dualities here, and no imperfections, either evident, apparent or supposed. All is perfection — perfect peace, perfect bliss, perfect wisdom and perfect freedom. Fully adept masters of the dance inhabit this timeless realm. It is, in fact, the Advaitic state, the Divine Mother's own flow of illumined thought, Her own indrawn mood of transcendental meditation. No hint of disharmony ever penetrates this realm, for Truth alone shines here, revealing all conditional states to be without any abiding reality. This is the home of primal Spirit, where all beings ultimately abide. From this safe haven they may embark upon the dreams of relative existence or perform some divine function at the behest of the Universal Mother, but the obvious unreality of all such movement is clearly apparent. Such a state is impossible to convey to the mind caught in the net of duality, ensconced in relativity. It is a matter of direct experience only, for its nature is unified experience, eternal and absolute.

Another rendering of mukti is expressed in the *Srimad Devi Bhagavatam* and concurred with in the Vedas. Whereas the three kinds of mukti above are perceived and explained in terms of formless Reality, there are four kinds of mukti that come as a result of worshipping God with form. Although these are wonderful attainments, they are considered by the Bhaktas to be of secondary importance to the attainment of pure devotion, sought after only as a benefit to possessing that rare treasure. As the *Devi Bhagavatam* explains:

Mukti is of four kinds: Salokya, Sarupya, Samipya and Sayujya. So it is stated in the Vedas. Out of them, devotion for the Lord is the highest, so much so that it is considered superior even to mukti. Mukti gives Salokya, Sarupya, Samipya and Sayujya, but the true devotees desire more than this. They want service of the Lord and nothing else. The state of becoming immortal, a god, of transcending birth, death, suffering, old age and disease, of gaining wealth, of assuming a divine form, of receiving moksha — the attainment of these are looked upon by true bhaktas with disregard and contempt. This is because mukti is without service, while bhakti increases service! This is the difference between bhakti and mukti.

This wonderful teaching is in keeping with a new standard of inspired thinking in terms of spiritual perception in this age, a standard set by the appearance of Sri Ramakrishna, Sri Sarada Devi, Swami Vivekananda, and the disciples and devotees of these three great beings. Service of God in humanity is not only practical, sensible and kind, it is also wise, for the Blessed Lord dwells in all beings. As the *Purusha Stuti* declares, rightly and adamantly: *"Salutations to my God, with thousands of eyes, thousands of legs and thousands of arms, covering the entire universe."* The lesson delivered by the scriptures after this fashion tallies with all the expressions of ancient wisdom and applies to every facet of spiritual life. Without devotion, nothing has meaning: knowledge is futile, service is without cause, the practice of sadhana has no reason, the study of the scriptures bears no appreciable fruit and meditation has no objective. In this sense, one can rightly understand Thakur Sri Ramakrishna Paramahamsa's famous declaration, *"Bhakti Yoga is the path for this age."*

It is not to be inferred by these statements that liberation is a low ideal. On the contrary, it is to be sought after by beings caught up in relative existence with all the strength and energy that can be mustered. Indeed, all sadhanas must be undertaken for this reason, for a balanced and exemplary spiritual life is the result. For the consummate devotee though, the attainment of spiritual emancipation simply for the sake of personal freedom, the likes of which leaves others to fend for themselves, stranded in a web of suffering and deception, is undesirable. Sarva Mukti, liberation for all, is not possible so to speak, if all are not emancipated from their condition of bondage. For this reason, it is helpful to explore all the steps leading to the attainment of such sterling qualities as pure devotion.

Truthfully speaking, true bhakti grants mukti, but true knowledge aids in the attainment of bhakti and also leads to mukti as well. Few are those who are able to possess the burning faith and driving zeal needed to capture the true spirit of devotion immediately. Most beings must reach the differing stages of liberation first, through knowledge that destroys ignorance, experiencing a slow maturation of devotion along the way. In this process, the four types of emancipation called *Salokya, Sarupya, Samipya and Sayujya* are of great value. The first three are extremely sweet and coveted by all aspirants seeking union with the personal aspect of God. The fourth, often called *Nirvana,* is pivotal, being equated with the final immersion of the individual soul into the Supreme Being.

Salokya, attaining the same region as the Divine Being, is the very epitome of sweet salvation and more. With this type of liberation, the soul is able to abide in the same realm as the Lord, enjoying the presence of that particular personal ideal most cherished by the aspirant. This equates to heavenly existence, a state of bliss enjoyed for an interminable time, but it is not the enjoyment of a mere celestial realm full of pleasurable sensations as is the case with the lower heavens. This condition is attended by the divine form of the Beloved that is most dear to the devotee. Such a situation affords an ongoing period of spiritual growth for the seeker of Ultimate Reality, full of wisdom teachings and the maturation of pure love. Close communion of this nature with a direct manifestation of divinity speeds up the evolutionary process considerably and burns away all tendencies that may cause a return to a grosser embodied existence. Therefore, the extreme importance of such a state is appreciated greatly by the devotees.

A still higher condition is called *Sarupya,* defined as the attainment of the same form as God. The personal aspect of the Lord that is most cherished by the devotee becomes directly accessible in this mode, and the same status is enjoyed. Sri Ramakrishna's analogy of the devoted servant is applicable here. Lifelong service to the master of the house so enamors the servant to him that, one day, the master calls the servant to the study, asks him to sit in his own personal chair, feeds him with his own hands and offers to him the management of the family business — all of this despite the protestations of the surprised servant! In short, he has become one of the family and is treated from that moment forth in a most respectful fashion. Such an example illustrates the essence of Sarupya, reaching the same status as the chosen ideal.

If there is any higher attainment than these two wonderful kinds of liberation, it is the precious boon of becoming beloved of the Lord. The devotee loves the Lord, no doubt, but imagine the bliss of receiving the Blessed Lord's sweetest attentions. *Samipya*, experiencing the bliss of being extremely dear to God, is indescribable. It is akin to the spiritual mood of *Sakhya*, in which an abiding and eternal friendship with God is fully developed. The fortunate one who has the Supreme Being for a friend is indeed blessed, for all manner of attainments then become accessible, immediately and unconditionally! This is like having a wealthy and doting king for a father. No want or desire can ever go unfulfilled in this state. Therefore, the condition of Samipya is seen as the apex of all liberated states, being the fulfillment and coalescence of all previous levels of freedom and heralding the arrival of the much coveted position of total spiritual emancipation. This is called *Sayujya*, or *Nirvana*.

Sayujya accomplishes the release from any and all limitations of form but does not necessarily dictate a departure from the bliss of communion with divine forms. Whereas the unbound soul can traverse and explore the ocean of Consciousness, experiencing the inexpressible bliss of immersion into formless Reality, the experience of communion with any or all of the many divine forms which reside on the shores of the ocean of light is still possible. This makes the liberation called Sayujya one of absorbing delight. There is little wonder why it is equated with Nirvana, for the definition of the term Nirvana is to "blow out." In the case of this consummate liberation, all of the restricting waves or vibrations of limited mental states have been calmed or neutralized, leaving the flow or stillness of conscious Awareness unimpeded.

The Great Master, Sri Ramakrishna, expresses the unalloyed joy of such an infinite experience as follows: *"Imagine that you are a fish, suddenly released from the confines of a bowl into the boundless ocean."* Such unexpected and overwhelming freedom is exhilarating, and the fish is able to freely move about the infinite expanse of water while simultaneously beholding all the myriad forms inhabiting it. This analogy confers upon the mind's understanding a sense of the powerful and sublime nature of the experience of Sayujya. As mentioned earlier, this condition is complete, all-inclusive and lacking nothing. It contains the Peace cherished by all beings, the Bliss desired by all beings, the Truth sought after by all beings, the Love which fulfills all beings and is the perfect expression of unlimited Freedom that all are seeking.

Summary

Mother Kali – Deva Devi Svarupaya

Indivisible though consisting of infinite parts,
Transcendent yet pervading everything!

At the end of the dream journey of transmigrating consciousness, effected by the movement of individualized human awareness through the infinite realms of being and becoming — the many chambers of the Lord's mansion of perpetual existence — there abides the limitless Brahman, Mother Kali's formless essence. Sporting throughout the universe in a dynamic mode, the Divine Mother draws this sublime Essence from within Her and projects It into countless life forms. Despite this phenomenon, the formless Essence proves to be inseparable, indivisible. She fashions the cosmos, replete with three highly variegated worlds containing innumerable planes of existence, yet It remains untouched, unaffected and unmanifested. She transmits this boundless and immutable essence as energy at a multitude of differing levels of vibratory intensity, gross and subtle, but It remains impervious to all conditions and defies all tendencies or influences towards modification or diversification.

In short, the Divine Mother, as it were, grasps the uncontainable and spreads It across, around and through the very fabric of existence, like a delighted painter intent on covering a canvas with a diverse array of vibrant colors. Interpenetrating this spacious canvas in three modes — the Immanent, the Transcendent and the Absolute — She Herself appears in Her many astonishing aspects, some of which have been explored within the pages of this book.

The twenty-four powerful ways expressed herein, through which the primordial Goddess makes Her awesome and august presence known, are not mere symbolisms, for a symbol is only a secondary representation of the original. These aspects are not just external attributes or excellences either, like awards or merit badges pinned upon a sash, for Her eternal and sublime presence permeates and radiates through each one of them. Nor are these twenty-four aspects just expressions, conduits or powers through which Her ineffable Being can flow, for in Truth there can be no delineation, division or sequestering of Her formless essence.

There can be, then, only one conclusion: *Ever One, appearing as Two, and residing in the many without the slightest sense of separation* — *this is the Supreme Beloved.* Mother Kali's essence completely permeates the many, which are integral portions of It, and the many abide within It eternally. The Four Arms of Mother Kali, Her Wisdom Eye, Her Lotus Feet, Her Garland of Human Heads, Her Nakedness, Her Awesome Appearance, the Battlefield of Relativity, Her Waistband of Human Arms, the Blood of Sacrifice, Her Protruding Tongue, the Lightning Flashes from Her Teeth, the Crescent

Moon on Her Brow, Her Radiant Blackness, Her Long Black Flowing Hair, the Swarms of Bees about Her Hair, Her Female Attendants, Her Hairpiece Crown, the Anklets and Bracelets of Snakes, Her Demon and Jackal Companions, the Blessed Lord Shiva beneath her Feet and Her cosmic dance — all combine to convey an absolute sense of fullness, of all-pervasiveness, of all-inclusiveness.

Therefore, Brahman and Shakti, of an ancient and primal nature, timeless and deathless, are ever immersed in oneness, whether absorbed in rapturous meditation in a static and supine conditionless condition or plunged into playful diversification in a dynamic mode of expression. All around, on all sides, within and without, above and below, nothing but That exists and Its ineffable presence is found to be the essence in all. It is no wonder, then, that saints, sages and other illumined beings reverently declare:

> There is only this One, existing in all beings
> and all existing in It.
> It filters down and touches all hearts and minds,
> yet nothing can touch It.
> It is like the sky, pure and serene,
> subtle and impossible to taint.
> That One am I, I am that One,
> there can be none other.[28]

Notes

1   Ramprasad poem No. 21, translated by Lex Hixon, featured on the *Shakti Bhajans* album by Jai Ma Music.

2   From "The Song of the Sannyasin," in the collection *In Search of God and Other Poems*, by Swami Vivekananda, published by Advaita Ashrama.

3   Ibid.

4   This and the above quote are from Swami Vivekananda's song, "Achandala," written in Sanskrit. This English translation by Babaji Bob Kindler is found in the *Jai Ma Music Songbook, Vol. I.*

5   *In the Company of the Holy Mother*, Advaita Ashrama, pp. 357-58.

6   From "Sadanandamayi Kali," a Bengali devotional song by Kamalakanta, on the Jai Ma Music album, *Hymns to the Goddess*, and also in their Songbook. Translation by Babaji Bob Kindler.

7   This reference is to Swami Vivekananda's poem, "Hymn to the Divine Mother," which can be found in the collection entitled, *In Search of God and other Poems*, Advaita Ashrama.

8   Quotations from the songs of Ramprasad are from *Mother of the Universe* by Lex Hixon, unless otherwise noted.

9   Ramprasad poem no. 299 on the Jai Ma Music album, *The Ecstatic Songs of Ramprasad*, translation by Lex Hixon.

10 Ramprasad poem no. 215 on the Jai Ma Music album, *Shakti Bhajans*, translation by Lex Hixon.

11 *In Search of God and Other Poems*, Advaita Ashrama.

12 Ramprasad poem no. 213 on the Jai Ma Music album, *The Ecstatic Songs of Ramprasad*, translations by Lex Hixon.

13 Ibid., poem no. 259.

14 "Ma Ki Amar Kalo Re" by Kamalakanta, from the album, *Hymns to the Goddess*, Jai Ma Music. Translation by Babaji Bob Kindler.

15 *Sri Sarada Devi, the Holy Mother; Life and Conversations,* Swami Tapasyananda and Swami Nikhilananda, Sri Ramakrishna Math, Madras, 1977, p.289.

16 From "Hymn to the Divine Mother," *In Search of God and Other Poems,* by Swami Vivekananda, Advaita Ashrama.

17 Translation by Babaji Bob Kindler.

18 This is a reference to the path of Tantra in which *pasu* (animal), *virya* (heroic), and *daiva* (divine) are seen as ascending steps in the evolution of human awareness.

19 Ramprasad poem no. 17, Jai Ma Music album, *The Ecstatic Songs of Ramprasad,* translation by Lex Hixon.

20 Written by the author.

21 "Hymn to the Divine Mother," *In Search of God and Other Poems,* by Swami Vivekananda, Advaita Ashrama.

22 Quoted from *The Gospel of Sri Ramakrishna,* p. 122.

23 "Hymn to the Divine Mother," *In Search of God and Other Poems,* Swami Vivekananda, Advaita Ashrama.

24 *Neti neti* – "Not this, not this"; A method of discrimination that rejects what is unreal to find what is real. *Iti iti* – Literally, "all this, all this"; a phrase used to express the all-pervasive nature of Brahman.

25 *A Short Life of the Holy Mother,* by Swami Pavitrananda, Advaita Ashrama, 1980, p. 91.

26 Ramprasad poem no. 64, *The Ecstatic Songs of Ramprasad,* Jai Ma Music, translation by Lex Hixon.

27 Ibid.

28 From *Hasta Amalaka Stotram – A Hymn of Eternal Enlightenment,* translation and commentary by Babaji Bob Kindler, SRV Associations of Oregon, San Francisco & Hawaii.

Who is She?
A Few of Her Infinite Names

*The One Permeating the Many, the Many
Residing in the One*

Adishakti   The first, original primordial Goddess who
places in motion the cycles of universal manifestation,
projecting, sustaining and dissolving the world of
name and form at the appropriate time according to
Her perfect omniscience.

Ambika   A name for Mother Kali, especially sweet to Her
devotees and particularly associated with Her victorious exploits on the field of battle against powerful negative forces.

Bagala   One of the Dasamahavidyas, attendants of the
Divine Mother, and an aspect of Her concerned with
exposing and consuming the many detrimental
propensities that inhabit the human mind such as
anger, lust, jealousy, greed and all of the offshoots of
the negative passions.

Bhadra Kali   An aspect of the Universal Mother which is
gentle and pleasing to the devotees but wrathful in
appearance to the asuras (demons or demonic forces).
Her appearance is usually attended by many yoginis.

Bhagavati   One of the supreme names of the Divine
Mother; the Blessed Lord as Mother.

Bhairavi   One of the Dasamahavidyas, attendants of the
Divine Mother, who is powerful and terrible and whose
primary function is to reveal the distinctions between
good and evil, right and wrong and other pairs of opposites, thereby allowing them to be neutralized, bringing
back a peaceful balance to life in the universe.

Bhakti Devi   The Goddess residing within all beings as the essence of pure love for God; the divine consort or shakti of Vairagyam, the god of detachment and dispassion, who grants jivanmukti. (liberation)

Bhuvaneshwari   One of the Dasamahavidyas, attendants of the Divine Mother; a profound and special name for the Mother of the Universe revealing Her as the presiding deity of all things refined and subtle; The Mother of the celestial regions who confers blissful experiences upon the devotees.

Brahmani   The Divine Mother in Her role as the Creatrix; the divine consort or shakti of Lord Brahma.

Buddhi Devi   That aspect of the Universal Mother who resides in and permeates the faculty of intelligence and aids in the comprehension of abstruse and subtle matters; the divine consort or shakti of Jnana Deva, who saves beings from ignorance and its detrimental results.

Chamunda   A powerful name conferred upon Goddess Kali by Sri Durga after She destroyed the fearful demons named Chanda and Munda.

Chinnamasta   One of the Dasamahavidyas, attendants of the Divine Mother, who personifies inner strength and perseverance, confers the boon of confidence and dependence on the Self and demonstrates the truth of divine life and immortality.

Dakshina Devi   The divine consort or shakti of the god of sacrifice, granting auspicious circumstances for ceremonies and rituals and bringing to bear the successful outcome of all such undertakings. She is worshipped everywhere, for Her presence brings fruits, benefits and prestige to all the gods and goddesses as well as to priests and aspirants.

Daya Devi   The Universal Mother in Her aspect as the compassionate savior; the wife of Moha Deva who together grant hope and mercy.

Dhriti Devi   The divine consort or shakti of the great Kapila Deva. She grants boons associated with patience and fortitude.

Dhumavati   One of the ten Dasamahavidyas, attendants of the Divine Mother, whose name is associated with fire, smoke and ashes. She burns away all attachments to relative existence and allows beings to attain perfect renunciation.

Digambari   Literally, "clothed in space." This is a very revered name for Goddess Kali who wears as Her only vesture the fabric of space, representing Her formless nature as pure Consciousness.

Diksha Devi   Like Dakshina Devi, Diksha Devi presides over sacrifice and its rewards, especially in the arena of rites and rituals.

Durga   The first and foremost among Divine Mother aspects or emanations, being the essential power inherent in the Supreme Lord in all His manifestations.

Ganga   The Divine Mother presiding over the healing powers in water, revered by Hindus in particular as the form of the holy river Ganges in India.

Indrani   The divine consort or shakti of Indra, the chief of the gods.

Ishvari   A comprehensive aspect of the Universal Mother who appears as the chosen ideal of the devotees, abiding in their hearts and minds.

Jagadamba   A powerful and beloved aspect of the
Mother of the Worlds, used especially in reference to
Durga and Kali.

Kali   The essential Supreme Goddess in Her awesome
manifestation, who as the divine consort of Lord Shiva
in Tantricism, is the creator, preserver and destroyer of
the empirical process, the devourer of ignorance and
delusion and the essence of all gods and goddesses,
being the controller of the cosmic process and its various functions. She is also the Goddess of Time, which
perceives all things that experience birth, growth, disease, decay, old age and death, while always remaining
untouched by and detached from such transformations.

Kalika   An extension of the name Kali.

Kamala   A name for the goddess Lakshmi, particularly
associated with the Mother's incredible beauty and
powers of attraction, all based upon Her intrinsic and
perfect purity.

Kaumari   The divine consort or shakti of Kartikeya, the
son of Lord Shiva.

Kirti Devi   The divine consort or shakti of Sukarma, the
god of right action. She grants the boons of good
works accomplished in the proper spirit and the fame
and well-being which proceed from them.

Kriya Devi   The divine consort or shakti of Udyoga, the
god of enthusiasm and positivity. She confers the
power to work and the ability to make cogent decisions. She also supports rules and regulations.

Lajja Devi   The divine consort or shakti of the god of
good behavior. She is modest and indrawn, full of
purity and other sterling qualities; a name for Sri

Sarada Devi, the blessed divine consort of Sri Ramakrishna Paramahamsa, the Kali Avatar.

Lakshmi   One of the main aspects of the Universal Mother who is eternally pure and presides over the bestowal of wealth and abundance on all levels of existence.

Mahamaya   The Great Enchantress. The Divine Mother who sports as pure Consciousness in all forms and who projects the universe and gives it the appearance of Reality.

Mahashakti   The Great Shakti who is the ultimate dynamic power of Brahman, controlling all aspects of the three worlds — Immanent, Transcendent and Absolute.

Mahavidya Mahamaya Devi   A powerful and comprehensive name for the Universal Mother that refers to Her embodiment of the highest nondual knowledge and Her ability to delude, enchant or awaken all beings according to Her Supreme Will.

Maheshvari Kali   The aspect of Mother Kali who is meticulous in nature, powerful and able to destroy the universe with a glance and who is "effulgent like the combined light of a million suns." She is also the granter of the four fruits of life (Purusharthas).

Mahavidya   A name used for the Divine Mother Sarasvati, the Goddess of art and learning, who is one of the main aspects of Divine Mother Reality.

Manasa Devi   A chief female deity among the Nagas and Naginis, serpent gods and goddesses who reside in and preside over watery regions. She is a great ascetic and famed for Her depth of knowledge.

Mangala Chandika A subtle and beneficent aspect of the Divine Mother who is always engaged in doing good to others. Being an aspect of Mother Kali, She is capable of extremes and is loving and compassionate at the beginning of creation but destructive at the end of universal cycles.

Matangi One of the Dasamahavidyas, attendants of the Divine Mother, who is the very essence of the power of domination and control. She brings about the downfall of arrogance and lust for power, whether personified in a demonic manifestation or existing in the human mind.

Murti Devi The divine consort or shakti of Dharma Deva, she who grants rest and repose and gives appreciation for beauty and substance.

Narasimhi The divine consort or shakti of Narasimha, the half man, half lion god.

Nirguna Devi The transcendent aspect of the Divine Mother of the Universe who is beyond all pairs of opposites and who resides in nondual bliss and equipoise, conferring those qualities upon Her votaries.

Phalaharini Devi The bringer of the fruits of action who bestows all things sought after by living beings according to their inherent karmas.

Pratistha Devi The divine consort or shakti of Punya Deva. She presides over the powers of fame, notoriety and merit.

Punya Devi Like Her divine consort, She grants fame and celebrity to deserving beings and those who need to experience these qualities.

Purna Devi   An aspect of the Universal Mother who grants completion and abundance.

Pusti Devi   The divine consort or shakti of Sri Ganesha, she who provides nourishment and vigor to all beings.

Radha   The divine consort of Lord Krishna and one of the five main aspects of Divine Mother Reality who embodies the very essence of pure love and unalloyed devotion.

Rajasika Devi   The Divine Mother who presides over the activity of all beings and who infuses the universe with motion and momentum.

Sampatti Devi   The divine consort or shakti of Ishana Deva. She is worshipped by gods and men alike for the boon of physical and mental well-being. Her presence grants refuge from poverty and hunger.

Sarasvati   The Supreme Goddess of Art and Knowledge who is one of the main aspects of Divine Mother Reality. She is ancient and primordial, even by historical standards, since Her name is found in the ancient Vedic scriptures.

Sati Devi   The divine consort or shakti of Satya Deva, the god of Truth. She is precious to those who have achieved liberation and She provides friendship and grants love of Truth.

Sattvika Devi   The Divine Mother who presides over the balance of all things in the universe, providing all beings with the opportunity for enlightenment.

Savitri   The Supreme Goddess in Her aspect that confers the comprehension of holy names, mantras and other branches (*angas*) of specialized knowledge upon sincere seekers. She is one of the five main aspects of Divine Mother Reality.

Shankari   the divine consort or shakti of Lord Shiva, Shankara, who is equipped with all His powers and wisdom. She is known for Her great asceticism.

Shanti Devi   Like Lajja Devi, Shanti Devi is the divine consort or shakti of the god of good behavior. She bestows upon Her votaries sanity, fulfillment and a peaceful nature.

Shasthi Devi   An important aspect of the Divine Mother who quietly and protectively watches over children. Beings worship Her for the birth of sons and daughters.

Shodashi   Literally, "eternally sixteen." This revered aspect of the Universal Mother is associated with purity, chastity, youthful vigor and eternal life in the Spirit.

Shraddha Devi   Like Bhakti Devi, Shraddha Devi is the divine consort or shakti of Vairagyam and grants fulfillment and spiritual emancipation.

Svadha Devi   She is the divine consort or shakti of Agni, the god of fire, and grants the fruits of sacrifices and oblations offered at the time of homa and other ceremonies.

Svaha Devi   The wife of the ancestors (*pitris*) who grants auspiciousness to departed spirits transmigrating to other realms of existence.

Svasti Devi   The divine consort or shakti of Vayu, the god of the wind. She allows the fructification of all undertakings and is found to be the essence of giving and receiving.

Tamasika Devi   The Divine Mother who presides over the destruction of the creation at the time of universal dissolution.

Tara   One of the ten Dasamahavidyas, attendants of the Divine Mother, who is subtle, boundless transcendent, yet whose compassion for all beings has become legend.

Tripura Sundari   The Divine Mother as the combined essence of three goddesses who personify protection and sustanence of the three worlds. Their beauty is beyond comprehension.

Tulsi   A very important aspect of the Divine Mother who heals the creation and who embodies pure and unswerving faith and devotion in the Supreme Lord.

Tusti Devi   The divine consort or shakti of Ananta Deva, the lord of the Nagas (serpent gods), she who confers satisfaction and contentment.

Vaishnavi   The divine consort or shakti of Vishnu, she who is the power of preservation and the refuge of the gods.

Varahi   The divine consort or shakti of the boar god, Varaha, she who uses departed spirits (pretas) for Her mounts.

Vasundhara   A beloved aspect of the Universal Mother who presides over all things of the earth, particularly the bounty of foodstuffs, precious metals and other necessities which sustain life and well-being.

Glossary

Abhaya mudra – A mystical gesture which confers fearlessness.

Achintya – Incomprehensible; impossible to conceive with the mind.

Adharma – Unrighteousness; imbalance of thought, word, deed, lifestyle.

Advaita – Nondual philosophy of absolute unity without compromise, brought into prominence by the great philosopher Adishankaracharya.

Advaita Vedanta – Nondual Truth; a system of philosophy propounded by Gaudapada and Shankaracharya.

Advaitan – One who lives by and subscribes to the Advaita philosophy.

Advaitic – Nondual in content; of the nature of nonduality and having to do with Advaita Philosophy.

Ajna chakra – One of seven subtle spiritual centers, itself being located at the throat region.

Ananda – The transcendent bliss of Pure Consciousness.

Ananta – Infinity; the snake upon which Lord Vishnu rests.

Antaryami – God as the internal guide enshrined within the heart; the "inner ruler immortal."

Anubhava – Direct perception of Divinity, which is the result of self-effort and Grace.

Archa – Objects of worship and their names; offerings made at the time of worship.

Artha – Attainment of wealth; right livelihood; one of the four fruits of life (Purusharthas) granted by the Divine Mother.

Asuras – Powerful beings who vie for supremacy with the gods; negative forces or demons.

Atman – The eternal Soul residing within every being, which is birthless, deathless, pure and perfect by nature.

Aum – The sacred symbol for Brahman; the soundless sound or primordial vibration of pure Existence.

Avatar – One who descends; the appearance of Divinity in human form; an incarnation of God.

Avidya Maya – The deluding power of Maya that leads away from illumination and towards ignorance.

Avidya Shakti – The power of Shakti that restricts rather than aids in the attainment of enlightenment.

Bhagavan – An especially sacred name for God.

Bhagavati – The Supreme Being manifest as the Mother of the Universe.

Bhakta – A devotee of the Lord; a follower of the path of Bhakti.

Bhakti – Devotion for the Supreme Lord.

Bhakti Yoga – The path of devotion leading to union with God.

Bhuh (or Bhur) – The earthly plane of existence.

Bhuh/Bhuvah/Suvah (or Svahah) – The earthly, etheric and heavenly planes of existence, sometimes described as physical, astral and causal. They are three of the seven Vyahrtis – sacred syllables representing the seven upper worlds. (See the Taittiriyopanisad, chapter one.)

Bhuvah – The celestial regions or life-heavens.

Brahma – The first aspect of the Hindu Trinity who represents the power of creation.

Brahman – The Absolute; the Ultimate Reality; formless essence.

Buddhi – Intelligence; one of the four portions of Antahkarana, the mental sheath or human mind according to Samkhya and Vedanta.

Chaitanya – Pure and Absolute Consciousness without modifications that knows all things.

Chakra – Spiritual vortex or center, of which there are seven according to the science of Kundalini Yoga, located in the subtle body associated with the spinal column; a divine weapon particularly associated with

Vishnu and His primordial Shakti.

Chandi – *The Devi Mahatmyam.* A holy scripture of over 700 mantrams describing and pertaining to the Divine Mother of the Universe.

Dasamahavidyas – Ten Divine Attendants of the Divine Mother; aspects of Mother reality.

Daya – Compassion, especially associated with the removal of suffering and specifically the ignorance which causes it.

Desha – Physical space; locale.

Desha/Kala/Nimitti – Space, time and causation.

Devas – The gods who reflect the powers of the Supreme Being.

Deva Devi Svarupaya – The essence of all gods and goddesses; a name for Mother Durga and Mother Kali.

Devi Mahatmyam – One of the authoritative sacred texts of Divine Mother worship.

Devis – The goddesses who reflect the powers of the Supreme Being.

Dharma – Proper and balanced living and thinking according to the scriptures; righteousness; virtue; one of the four fruits of life (Purusharthas) granted by the Divine Mother.

Durga – The Divine Mother of the Universe; the ten-armed Goddess who is the essence of all gods and goddesses; the first of five main aspects of the Universal Mother (Prakriti Panchaka) according to the *Srimad Devi Bhagavatam.*

Durgasaptasati – The many collected mantras pertaining to Sri Durga; also called the *Devi Mahatmyam* and the *Chandi.*

Dvaita – Dualistic philosophy; diversity; two or many.

Dvara-pala – Guardians or protectors, usually associated with temples and shrines.

Ganga – The Goddess of sacred waters whose powers aid in purification and transformation; the holy river located in India, revered by all Hindus.

Garuda – The great dragon bird who is Lord Vishnu's royal mount.

Gunas – Sattvas, rajas and tamas – perfect balance, frenetic activity and inertia; the three modes, qualities or attributes of nature.

Hiranyagarbha – Cosmic mind; the highest created being (Brahma) through which the Supreme Being projects the physical universe; the cosmic prana.

Indra – The Lord of the gods; the foremost among the lesser powers of the Supreme Being.

Indrani – The divine consort or shakti of Indra, the chief of the gods.

Ishta – The chosen ideal; that which the devotee accepts as the highest standard in spiritual life.

Ishvara – The supreme and most comprehensive aspect of divinity residing within the universe who oversees its various lesser powers and their functions.

Ishvari – The supreme power of the universe in a feminine aspect.

Iti-iti – Literally, all this, all this. A phrase used to express the all-pervasive nature of Brahman.

Itihasa – Spiritual history and mythology of India, especially reflected in the *Mahabharata, Ramayana* and other famous texts.

Jagadamba – The Divine Mother who pervades the worlds.

Jiva – Embodied soul possessing a sense of ego; individualized consciousness.

Jnana – Knowledge; spiritual wisdom associated with the path of discrimination which benefits spiritual life.

Jnana Yoga – The path of wisdom leading to union with the Supreme Being.

Kaivalya – Spiritual emancipation; absolute independence or transcendence, synonymous with the terms moksha or mukti, used particularly by Patanjali in his Yoga system.

Kala – Time; black; a name associated with Lord Shiva.

Kali – A supreme name for the Divine Mother of the Universe as the Deva Devi Svarupaya – the essence of all gods and goddesses; She who personifies time and acts as a witness to the phenomenal march of events contained in it; the Divine Mother of the Universe in Her four-armed form, worshipped by Sri Ramakrishna Paramahamsa; Lord Shiva's dynamic power and eternal consort.

Kalpataru – The wish-fulfilling tree that grants boons to the devotees.

Kama – Fulfillment of legitimate desires; one of the four fruits of life (Purusharthas) granted by the Divine Mother.

Karandamukuta – The hairpiece crown worn by gods and goddesses.

Karma – Good and bad action and its results; residual effects appearing in the life of embodied beings due to past and present activities.

Karma Yoga – The path of selfless service and divinely oriented action.

Karma yogini/yogi – One who is perfect in works and ever free from their effects.

Kartikeya – One of the sons of Lord Shiva, often called Skanda or Subramuniya.

Kundalini – The powerful yet subtle spiritual force that when awakened brings illumination to all levels of being.

Kundalini Yoga – The path which concentrates upon awakening the kundalini power at the base of the spine.

Lila – Play or sport, especially associated with consciousness appearing in the universe.

Mahadeva – The great god, often used as an epithet for Lord Shiva.

Mahakala – The Divine Mother Kali in Her supreme condition; the powerful aspect of time as the great witness of all phenomena.

Mahalila – The great play or sport of consciousness; the cosmic theatre with all beings as actors and actresses.

Mahamaya – The grand illusion; the superimposition of the universe and its constituents over Brahman; the One who conjures up the grand illusion.

Mahashakti – The great Shakti in Her role of creator, preserver and destroyer of the universe of name and form.

Mahavidya – Supreme wisdom; a name for the goddess Sarasvati, the Mother of learning.

Matapatha – The Divine Mother path.

Matrika – A form or aspect of the Divine Mother of the Universe.

Maya – Illusion; the projecting and veiling power of Brahman which causes the appearance and disappearance of the universe.

Moksha – Spiritual emancipation.

Mudra – A mystical hand gesture that represents and transmits specific powers or qualities.

Mukti – Liberation of the bound soul.

Mula Prakriti – Literally, root nature. The foundation of the created universe implying its Creator, in this case, the Divine Mother of the Universe, the source and origin of all manifestation.

Nagas – Male serpent gods possessing great powers such as healing and protection; a class of sadhu who are completely nude.

Naginis – Same as Nagas only of the female gender.

Narasimha – A god who is half lion, half man.

Narasimhi – The consort or divine shakti of Narasimha.

Narayana – A name for God; God manifest in mankind.

Neti-neti – Not this, not this; A method of discrimination that rejects what is unreal to find what is real.

Nimitta – Causation or causality; the vehicle or instrument which is the manifestation of a cause.

Nirguna – Formless; completely devoid of qualities or

attributes.

Nirguna Brahman – The Supreme Being as the highest condition of awareness, beyond name and form and without modifications or attributes.

Nirguna Devi – The Supreme Goddess in Her aspect of
formless Consciousness, absolute and supine.

Nirvana – Literally, to blow out or extinguish; liberation;
nondual experience characterized by the cessation of
mental activity.

Nirvikalpa samadhi – Nondual experience; immersion into
formless essence.

Niskama karma – Action accomplished with no selfish
motive, therefore having no resultant effect on the agent.

Nitya – Absolute; formless; eternal; permanent.

Om or Aum – The quintessential bija mantra epitomizing
transcendent perfection; the unstruck sound or primal
vibration from which the creation springs.

Param – That which is supreme.

Prakriti – Nature; causal matter; the universe of name and
form and those ingredients which comprise it; the
pradhana of Samkhya which corresponds to the Maya
of Vedanta with these main distinctions – it has its own
existence and it is considered real.

Prakriti Panchaka – An appellation referring to the Divine
Mother of the Universe as the five main powers of
Shakti who together constitute Divine Reality in its
dynamic mode. The five aspects are Durga, Lakshmi,
Sarasvati, Savitri and Radha.

Pralaya – Dissolution of the phenomenal universe after an
extremely long cycle of time.

Prana – Subtle energy; life-force; vital being; the subtle
force from which all mental and physical energy has
evolved.

Pretas – Disembodied spirits caught between physical and
astral realms.

Puranas – Ancient Vedic scriptures, eighteen in number,

illustrating the lives of Avatars, saints and sages and those who came in contact with them.

Purna – Fullness; completeness.

Purna Yogis – Thoroughly illumined beings adept at all aspects of Yoga.

Purusha – The Absolute Reality abiding in the hearts of all beings.

Purushartas – The four fruits of life – dharma, artha, kama and moksha.

Raja Yoga – The royal path; in reference to Patanjala Yoga which facilitates mastery of meditation and attainment of samadhi.

Rajas – One of the three gunas that compels beings towards desire-motivated activity.

Rajasika – Rajasic in nature; active and motivated by personal gain.

Rajasika Devi – The Divine Mother in Her aspect that presides over all activity and those who assume the responsibility of agency for their actions.

Raktabija – Literally, drop of blood; a unique and terrible demon, destroyed by Mother Kali, that could reproduce itself identically from every drop of blood that spilled from its veins.

Ramakrishna Paramahamsa – The Kali Avatar who was the God-realized master of 19th century India, generally accepted as the Divine Incarnation of this age.

Ramprasad – A Bengali poet/saint of the 14th century who was a devotee of Mother Kali and whose songs inspired many beings including Sri Ramakrishna Paramahamsa, who used them to illustrate spiritual truths.

Sadhana – Spiritual disciplines undertaken to realize God.

Sahasrara chakra – The spiritual vortex at the crown of the head associated with complete enlightenment; the crown chakra.

Sakhya – A mood or attitude assumed by a devotee which looks upon God as friend or companion.

Salokya – Abiding in the same plane, realm or world with the Lord.

Samadhi – Supersensual spiritual experience.

Samipya – Exceedingly dear to the Lord while enjoying God's direct presence.

Samsara – Life lived in cyclic rounds of ignorance, subject to suffering and delusion.

Samskaras – Positive and negative latent impressions in the subconscious and unconscious mind that shape human character, caused by repetitious actions through many lifetimes.

Sarada Devi – The Divine Mother in human form manifesting in this age, also known as the Holy Mother, the spiritual consort of Sri Ramakrishna Paramahamsa.

Sarupya – Being of the same form as God

Satchidananda – Pure Being, pure Consciousness, pure Bliss absolute; a name for the formless Brahman.

Sattva guna – Sattvas; the mode of Prakriti that induces balance and equilibrium.

Sayujya – Attaining oneness with Divine Reality.

Shakti – The creative force of the universe which is the active principle of Brahman yet identical with It.

Shakti-chaitanya – Dynamic Consciousness in a creative mode.

Shiva – The third deity in the Hindu Trinity; the God of wisdom who dissolves the universe of name and form at the end of cosmic cycles.

Shrutis – A comprehensive name for the primary scriptures emphasizing that they are revealed and authoritative.

Shunya – Void; nothingness.

Smriti – Memory; code of law; auxiliary scriptures supporting the Vedas and Upanishads (shruti).

Swami Vivekananda – The foremost disciple of Sri Ramakrishna, called an incarnation of the Buddha and of Lord Shiva by many. He is responsible for, among many other things, giving lucid contemporary interpretations to the ancient scriptures and spreading them broadcast throughout the world.

Tamas (Tamo guna) – The mode of Prakriti that induces slothfulness and inertia.

Tamasika – Having to do with the tamo guna.

Tantra – Auxiliary scriptures (Agamas) based upon the Vedas and dedicated to Vishnu, Shiva and the Divine Mother.

Tantra marga – The path of Tantric sadhana and practice of its disciplines.

Tantric – Having to do with Tantricism.

Tattvas (24 Cosmic Principles) – Cosmic principles; in Samkhya philosophy, a term for twenty-four constituents of Prakriti which make up the universe of name and form.

Titiksha – Forbearance and patience in spiritual practice; ability to bear all extremes, whether of a physical or mental nature; one of the Six Treasures of Vedanta practice.

Upadhi – Sheath or covering; a superimposition or limiting adjunct which appears to modify Absolute Reality. For example, a distant mountain range seems to lend its particular shape to formless space.

Upanishads – The Brahmakanda portion of the Vedas dealing with the knowledge that confirms Truth and reveals the Atman.

Varada mudra – A mystical hand gesture by which Divine Beings confer boons upon the devotees.

Vashishtadvaita – Qualified nondualism founded by Ramanuja, declaring that all beings are parts of God and that affirms the truth that God is real and the world is also real since God has created it and entered into it as consciousness.

Vedanta – One of the six traditional philosophies and orthodox darshanas of India, also called Uttara Mimamsa.

Vedantic – Having to do with Vedanta and its subjects.

Vedas – The four ancient scriptures of Sanatana Dharma which are eternal, without beginning and not ascribable to human authorship.

Vishnu – The second deity in the Hindu Trinity; the God of preservation and the one from whom the Avatars emerge.

Viveka – Discrimination; one of the Four Jewels of Vedanta practice.

Vyasa – A great and revered sage who composed the Brahma Sutras and who compiled the Vedantic scriptures at a certain point in time, considered as the father of the Uttara Mimamsa philosophy (Vedanta).

Yakshas – Beings under the influence of hoarding wealth; devotees of Kubera, the god of wealth.

Yama – The god of death in Hinduism. The cosmic law or energy in charge of shifts in transitional states from one relative condition to another.

Yoga – Union with Reality; a system of philosophy founded by Patanjali, often called Patanjala, Raja Yoga or Ashtanga Yoga (eight limbed).

Yogi/Yogini – A man or woman who succeeds in the path of Yoga.

Sources & Books
For Further Reading

Srimad Devi Bhagavatam, adeptly translated by Swami Vijnanananda. This amazing book of over 1000 pages is one of the few quintessential scriptures on the Divine Mother. We are sincerely grateful for Swami Vijnanananda's tremendous effort and contribution by translating this important text, and to the publishers for making it available for the Western devotees of the Divine Mother. Published by Munshiram Manoharlal Publishers Pvt. Ltd. P.O. Box 5715, 54 Rani Jhansi Road, New Delhi 110 055

Devi Mahatmyam, also known as the *Chandi,* a collection of 700 mantras in praise of the Divine Mother of the Universe. This scripture is available in many translations and concerns Mother Durga's victorious campaigns against the negative forces (Asuras).

Mother of the Universe, Visions of the Goddess and Tantric Hymns of Enlightenment, by Lex Hixon, Quest Books. These are expanded translations of songs to the Divine Mother, by Ramprasad Sen, a poet/saint of Bengal from the 14th century.

The Ecstatic Songs of Ramprasad, vol. I, Shakti Bhajan, and Hymns to the Goddess. The inspiring poetry of Ramprasad and Kamalakanta, is set to music and/or sung on these albums by Jai Ma Music. In addition to the above, this Sacred Arts Ensemble offers many more such albums and the *Jai Ma Music Songbook,* all featuring sacred chants and hymns with translations. Jai Ma Music P.O.Box 380, Paauilo, HI 96776

In Search of God and Other Poems, By Swami Vivekananda, Advaita Ashrama. This collection of poems and translations includes the famous poems "Kali the Mother," "Hymn to the Divine Mother," "Let Shyama Dance There," and others.

The Complete Works of Swami Vivekananda, Advaita Ashrama. The poems mentioned above and all other writings of the renowned Swami are included in this set of 9 volumes that presents the vast scope of Sanatana Dharma (Eternal Truth) for the modern age.

Bhagavad Gita, Among the many good translations and commentaries, we like to recommend Swami Chidbhavananda's, published by Sri Ramakrishna Tapovanam.

The Upanishads form the Brahmakanda portion of the Vedas which deal with the Knowledge that confirms Truth and reveals the Atman. The Upanishads are available individually or in combined volumes. We like to recommend those published by the various Sri Ramakrishna ashrams. The Upanishads referred to in this book are: *Mundako Upanishad, Katho Upanishad,* and *the Mahanarayana Upanishad.*

Self-Knowledge,(Atmabodha), by Shankaracharya, translation and commentary by Swami Nikhilananda. Swami Nikhilananda's introduction to this classic nondual text is an excellent resource for students of Sanatana Dharma (Eternal Truth). Published by the Ramakrishna-Vedanta Center, New York.

Ashtavakra Samhita, translation and commentary by Swami Nityaswarupananda, Advaita Ashrama.

Avadhuta Gita, translation and commentary by Swami Ashokananda, Sri Ramakrishna Math, Madras.

The biographies listed below depict the lives of beings who had the full realization of "Brahman as tangible as a fruit in the palm of the hand." As such, their words and their actions, as much as their teachings, are revealing and instructive to those desiring to live in Truth.

The Gospel of Sri Ramakrishna, recorded by "M" and translated by Swami Nikhilananda, Ramakrishna-Vedanta Center, New York.

Great Swan, Meetings with Ramakrishna, by Lex Hixon, Shambhala Press.

Sri Ramakrishna, the Great Master, by Swami Saradananda, Sri Ramakrishna Math, Madras.

Holy Mother, by Swami Nikhilananda, Ramakrishna-Vivekananda Center, New York.

The Gospel of the Holy Mother, Sri Sarada Devi, recorded by Her devotee-children, Sri Ramakrishna Math, Madras.

Teachings of Sri Sarada Devi, the Holy Mother, Sri Ramakrishna Math, Madras. This useful book lists the teachings of Holy Mother and provides the sources from which they are drawn.

Vivekananda, A Biography, by Swami Nikhilananda, Advaita Ashrama.

Talks with Swami Vivekananda, Advaita Ashrama.

The Eternal Companion — Brahmananda, His Life and Teachings, by Swami Prabhavananda, Vedanta Press, Hollywood.

Those interested in the wisdom teachings of the Divine Mother Path and Sanatana Dharma are invited to write, e-mail or phone SRV.

website: www.SRV.org
e-mail: SRVorg@teleport.com

SRV Oregon*
P.O. Box 14012
Portland, OR 97293
(503) 774-2410

SRV Hawaii
P.O. Box 380
Paauilo, HI 96776

SRV San Francisco*
465 Brussels Street
San Francisco, CA 94134
(415) 468-4680

SRV New England
1130 South Rd.
Hopkinton, NH 03229
(603) 746-4200

* If books are unavailable at local bookstores, they can be ordered from SRV Oregon or SRV San Francisco.

Other Books by the Author

We Are Atman All-Abiding

Strike Off Thy Fetters

Hasta Amalaka Stotram

The Ten Divine Articles of Sri Durga

The Avadhut and His Twenty-Four Teachers in Nature

Sri Sarada Vijnanagita